THE WORLD'S
STUPIDEST
Deaths

THE WORLD'S STUPIDEST
Deaths

**Andrew John
and
Stephen Blake**

Michael O'Mara Humour

First published in Great Britain in 2005 by
Michael O'Mara Books Limited
9 Lion Yard
Tremadoc Road
London SW4 7NQ

A CIP catalogue record for this book is available from the British Library

ISBN 1-84317-136-8

1 3 5 7 9 10 8 6 4 2

Designed and typeset by Design 23

Printed and bound in Great Britain by Cox & Wyman, Reading, Berks

Contents

Introduction

It's a funny old thing, death. Or at least it can be. It's not funny for those accomplishing it, however, as they know nothing about it once it's happened, and so can't share in the moment. Nor is it usual for loved ones to see the funny side of death, unless they have a starring role in the will, and then they can laugh all the way to the bank. But perhaps we shouldn't otherwise take death so seriously. After all, as so much gallows humour has proved over the centuries, being able to laugh about death helps us to cope with our knowledge of its inevitability.

Fortunately, for those of us who wish or need to have a giggle about the phenomenon in life that is as certain as taxes (to paraphrase Benjamin Franklin), there are numerous amusing stories concerning death and dying: those who have done it to themselves in spectacularly stupid ways; those who have done it to others likewise; those who have been just darned unfortunate. Yes, even they can leave us clutching our abdomens. As Oscar Wilde said in a lecture on Dickens, 'One would have to have a heart of stone to read the death of Little Nell without laughing.'

There have been mindless homicides for the most bizarrely trivial of reasons; baffling bravado that has left spectators wondering whether to phone for an ambulance or crease up in hysterics; crimes that have brought their own sweet justice to their perpetrators. Let's face it, when your time's up, you might as well shuffle off this mortal coil in a uniquely amusing manner that your friends can talk about over dinner for years to come.

With the caveat that you should definitely not try any of these at home, we have brought together some of the most hilarious or just plain mind-boggling stories about how people through the ages have met their ends, whether in the guise of historical figures or your everyday regular guy just doing something extremely stupid.

'Death . . . it's the only thing we haven't succeeded in completely vulgarizing!' wrote Aldous Huxley in his 1936 novel, *Eyeless in Gaza*. Well, you'll find plenty of vulgarization here. History books are full of noble deaths, but this collection features an array of deaths that are anything but noble: stupid deaths, asinine deaths, bizarre deaths, silly, childish and somewhat unwise deaths, deaths from fooling about, deaths from food and drink, the sillier deaths caused by crime, the weirder deaths in history, in sport and among friends and family.

In fact, this is a book that allows you to wallow in death – but be warned: you could die laughing!

Andrew John and Stephen Blake

Animal Tragic

Humans throughout history have enjoyed a relationship with animals – sometimes symbiotic, sometimes fatal. We have found a few of the fatal ones.

Bacon stuffing

Francis Bacon (1561–1626) was a politician, philosopher, historian, writer and scientist – and a stuffer of chickens. It was his involvement in the latter activity that is said to have led to his death.

The great man had applied his fecund mind to the preservation of meat, and while watching a snowstorm he began to wonder whether packing snow into a chicken would have the effect of preserving it. One day, when passing a snowy field near Highgate, north London, Bacon decided to put his theory to the test.

After stopping his coach, he bought a bird, killed it, gutted it and stuffed it with snow. He never found out whether the seventeenth-century equivalent of the deep freeze did the trick, because he caught a nasty chill during the experiment and had to seek refuge at the home of a friend, the Earl of Arundel, where he was invited to stay in a damp bedroom. He later died of pneumonia.

A Dasch to the death

It is said that people often open their big mouths at the wrong time, but when large animals do it the result can be fatal, as the unfortunate Austrian dwarf and circus acrobat Franz Dasch was to discover in July 1999. After executing a spectacular bounce from a trampoline, he landed in the mouth of a nearby hippo that was yawning at the time. It was thought at the time that the animal suffered a gag reflex, and so ingested the hapless Dasch.

What made matters worse was that the 7,000-plus spectators at the event in northern Thailand thought this astounding feat was all part of the show. It's amazing what some people will swallow . . .

The man it was that died

If you're stupid enough to attack a poor dumb creature with the stock of your gun, you probably deserve what's coming to you.

It would seem that this was what a forty-three-year-old man was up to in the US state of Virginia, in 2003, after the family's 30-pound Shar Pei had bit him.

He first phoned his wife at work to tell her that the dog had bitten him and that he intended to kill it, and when she arrived home at around 6 p.m. she found her husband unconscious, covered in dog bites and scratches – and bearing a fatal gunshot wound.

A police captain told reporters that the man had apparently been beating the dog with the stock of the combined shotgun and rifle when it went off. The stock was found to be broken, and it appeared to have blood and dog hair on it. The dog later went into the custody of an animal control officer.

Such sweet sorrow

Not satisfied with getting totally drunk one day in September 2003, a sixty-year-old man in Escobedo, Mexico decided that he might also like to try a bit of honey.

The trouble was that he went to a nest of bees to get it, and the occupants were not exactly chuffed. They did what evolution has equipped them to do, and fiercely protected their hive. Before he knew what was happening, more than a thousand worker bees had begun attacking him. He duly went into anaphylactic shock and died.

A hospital spokesman said it was not the bees alone that had killed the unidentified man, but 'the stupid things drunken people do', remarking that 'the combination was lethal.'

Cock-sure

Cockfighting is understandably illegal in many countries. It's a cruel and barbaric so-called sport. It's popular in the Philippines, however, and much money is gambled on the outcome of a good scrap between two belligerent cocks, each fitted with razor-sharp spurs to supplement its claws.

Thus a trained cock is a deadly weapon – not only to other cocks, but also to humans, as proven by an incident that occurred in January 2003 at a fight in Zamboanga in the southern Philippines.

The owner of a vicious cock became the target of his own bird, moments after he'd attached the lethal spurs. He lost control of the creature and it turned on him, slicing through major arteries in his groin and thigh. Despite being a seasoned cock owner, he had failed to wear any protective clothing, and such were his injuries that he had bled to death before making it to hospital.

Getting rattled by bad manners

We all know that it's rude to stick your tongue out at someone, but you wouldn't argue with a snake that did it – unless you were the drunken twenty-year-old man in California in 1992 who took umbrage at a rattlesnake's apparent lack of good manners.

The reason a snake sticks out its tongue is to pick up odours, which it then transports to the roof of its mouth, where there is a sensory receptor called the Jacobson's organ – but it would appear that our man didn't know that. Holding the disrespectful reptile right in front of his face, he decided to stick his own tongue out at this particular rattlesnake, after mistaking the creature's behaviour for discourtesy.

The snake was also a stickler for good manners, it seems, and took offence at this unseemly display, biting the man's tongue and injecting its toxic venom into it, causing it to swell, along with his face and throat, until he choked to death.

Snakes alive! (1)

Snakes have their own way of killing people and don't usually resort to guns, but in 1990 one Iranian reptile managed to do just that when it found itself pinned to the ground by a hunter.

Ali-Asghar Ahani had tried to catch the reptile alive by pressing his gun butt behind its head, but the trapped snake coiled itself around the shotgun and accidentally activated the trigger with its thrashing tail, killing its captor.

According to the Islamic Republic News Agency, another unnamed hunter tried to grab the shotgun, but the snake fired the other barrel in the same way. This man didn't meet the same fate as his hunting colleague, however, and managed to escape serious injury.

Into the lions' den

During the late 1980s a gullible martial-arts student was convinced that he could kill any wild animal. After all, his tutor had told him and his fellow students that they had now reached the point in their training at which they could perform such a feat. Being physically able to deliver a blow that will kill is one thing, but getting the intended victim to hold still while you line up your punch is quite another.

This student decided to put his newfound skills to the test, and one night stole into the Melbourne Zoo. How best to test his lethal skill? On a lion, of course – what else? So he went into the lions' enclosure and tried to take on one of its dangerous occupants. Unfortunately he didn't get to land a single blow, because the lion – totally unaware of the newly acquired lethal punching power of the intruder – attacked him first. The next day, all that was found of the misguided young man were two arms and two hands; the fingers poignantly grasping a few shreds of fur.

Raining dogs

A dog can bring joy, especially when it eagerly awaits its master's return, tail wagging, anticipating that scratch behind the ears so beloved of man's best friend. However, Araldo Anastasi's dog was just a bit too eager in the Via dello Scalo in Rome in 1954. On hearing his master approach the building – from four floors up – the over-excited pooch fell out of the apartment window and landed right on the old man's head.

The fate of the faithful dog is not recorded, but his unlucky owner paid the ultimate price. Talk about being dogged by bad luck!

Strictly from the birds

Strange, but true: an animal lover collapsed and died in Tegelen in the Netherlands in November 2003 after breathing in one too many parrot farts.

According to a story in the *Sun* newspaper, the unnamed victim had a double-glazed house that contained dozens of flapping, squawking parrots, and also reeked strongly of the expelled gases from his psittacine pals.

He was able to call for an ambulance before collapsing totally, but by the time the paramedics had arrived, it was too late. It was thought that death had been caused by the inhalation of both the parrots' gases and the ammonia from their droppings.

Perhaps one of the parrots took the unfortunate victim to the man shop and harangued the shop owner with, 'This is a dead man. It has ceased to exist. It has gone to join the choir invisible.'

Perhaps not.

Jumbo jobbie

Stefan was that most dangerous of elephants: a constipated one. In 1998, at Paderborn in west central Germany, a zookeeper called Friedrich Reisfeldt decided on a drastic diet to cure his pachyderm pal. He started with twenty-two doses of animal laxative, to which he then added more than a bushel of berries, prunes and figs. Surely anyone with any sense would know not to stand at the wrong end of such an afflicted animal when that end has so much potential to cause a mishap?

So it was that forty-six-year-old Reisfeldt found himself in the wrong place at the wrong time when the inevitable happened – and he ended up being suffocated under about 90 kilos of elephant poo.

A police detective, Erik Dern, told reporters, 'The sheer force of the elephant's unexpected defecation knocked Mr Reisfeldt to the ground, where he struck his head on a rock and lay unconscious as the elephant continued to evacuate his bowels on top of him.' The policeman revealed that Reisfeldt had lain there for at least an hour before a watchman came along and raised the alarm.

Snakes alive! (2)

Thirty-four-year-old Boonreung Bauchan managed to spend seven days locked up with poisonous snakes in 1998. In fact, he set a world record – and wasn't even harmed during the dangerous feat.

His demise came as a result of showing a new cobra to villagers in the north-eastern Thai province of Si Sa Ket in March 2004. He was bitten on the elbow, took some herbal medicine and a whisky, and carried on with the show. But Boonreung was an epileptic, and he later suffered severe convulsions before dying in Praibung hospital the next day.

Tiddles' revenge

The cat just wouldn't shut up. It miaowed, it howled, and drove fifty-five-year-old Giorgio Scrimin of Venice mad as he tried to get to sleep one night in autumn 1992.

Unable to stand the noise any longer, Scrimin grabbed a broom and leaned out of his bedroom window in the hope of hitting the maddening moggy to put an end to its infernal racket. The cat had other ideas, however, and as it leaped onto the roof of the house, it dislodged a lump of marble which fell on Signor Scrimin's head, killing him stone dead.

Demon Drink

The term 'demon drink' is usually associated with alcohol, but we came across a number of life-ending tales that feature drink in one way and another, though not all of it of the alcoholic variety. The stories are all deadly, though.

Ill met by moonlight

The great Chinese poet Li Bai (also known as Li Po, 707–62 CE) was a lover of all things natural, including the moon, and it was his passion for the moon, as well as his weakness for wine, that led to his death.

He was born into minor nobility in Szechwan province and took an apprenticeship with a Daoist hermit, before a brief spell as a poet at the royal court of the Tang dynasty in Changan. A minor intrigue caused him to leave his position at court, however, and he returned to reflective wandering, the writing of poems and the pleasures of wine, for he received free supplies of the stuff on the orders of the emperor.

Whether it was the case that he'd partaken of more than a few swigs of wine when he got into a boat and sailed out into the clear, moonlit night, we'll never know, but legend has it that he tried to embrace the reflection of the moon in the water – and promptly fell in and drowned.

Tell tale

A man called Larry and his lifelong friend Silas had consumed rather too much alcohol one day when they decided it would be a good idea to re-enact the famous William Tell trick of shooting an apple from a person's head. Tell had carried out the feat with his son using a crossbow; Silas, though, opted to aim at a beer can balanced precariously on Larry's head, and use a gun instead of a bow and arrow. In the event, however, he missed, and Larry was killed.

Although it was the sort of stunt that most people would associate with reckless teenagers, both Larry and Silas were grown men of forty-seven. Authorities were aware the men had been drinking, and, had ruled out the fact that an altercation in a nearby car park had had anything to do with the shooting.

Strong liquor

When used the wrong way, alcohol can be pretty dangerous, but in February 1992, when a thirty-five-year-old man from Ketchum, Idaho innocently opened his fridge in his garage, he wasn't expecting it to be quite that dangerous.

Unfortunately for him, a beer keg ruptured and shot upwards, hitting him in the head and killing him.

Crime Scene

Not surprisingly, many deaths occur as a result of crime, whether they are those you carry out yourself or those of which you're a victim – or just an unlucky bystander.

Decisions, decisions!

A series of very wrong and very stupid decisions ensured that a would-be thief in Washington State not only failed in his attempt to hold up a shop in February 1990, but also lost his life in the process.

Firstly, he chose the wrong target: H&J Leather & Firearms of Renton (near Seattle) was a gun shop; people who shopped there would have guns. Then there was the approach to the shop. The would-be robber actually had to step around a police car. How can you miss a marked police car when it's dressed up like a Christmas tree?

But it didn't end there. When he entered the shop, there was a uniformed cop having coffee at the counter before going to work. The wannabe robber saw the cop, announced that this was a hold-up and fired some random shots without hitting anyone. However, the policeman and the counter assistant returned fire, and the guns of several customers were also drawn. The criminal was thus fatally shot, and no one else was hurt.

Weighty crime

In 2002 a burglar in Tulsa, Oklahoma, stole more than he could carry, and it killed him. Had the thirty-seven-year-old criminal not jumped into a river in an attempt to evade capture by the police, he might still be alive to tell the tale – albeit from a prison cell.

After stuffing his duffel bag and his pockets full of booty, he jumped into the muddy Arkansas River to try to swim away from the pursuing cops, who suspected him of having robbed a Tulsa home. The weight of his stash was too much for him to bear, however, and proved to be his undoing.

A Tulsa police spokesman told reporters: 'He got about 40 yards [37 metres] out and yelled for help. The officers took off their shirts, shoes and belts and jumped into the river. By the time they reached him, he had gone under.'

The robber's body was found about an hour later – along with the bag and stolen goods.

Cockamamie

On 9 October 2003, Reuters news agency told the story of a twenty-eight-year-old man in Gambia, who was beaten to death for stealing in the town of Serekunda, about 9 miles (14 kilometres) from the capital, Banjul.

Nothing unusual in that, you may think, as in some parts of the world the crime of theft is still punishable by death, but the stolen item in this instance was another man's penis.

All is vanity

You can agonize over causal chains till the cows come home, but it is possible that the successful assassination of Francis Ferdinand, Archduke of Austria – which precipitated the Great War – can be linked to his narcissism.

Ferdinand was well known for his vanity, and, rather than allow one wrinkle to show on his smart uniform, he would have himself sewn into it. Consequently, when he was shot alongside his wife in Sarajevo, Bosnia, on 28 June 1914, those rushing to his aid could not find any buttons, and, by the time they had worked out how to cut off his tightly-fitting uniform, he had bled to death.

Dying for his art

Just as those actors who use the Method will go to great lengths to bring authenticity to their performance, so it is with some writers, it seems. All writers need to do research, but fifty-five-year-old author Jack Drummond took it a tad too far.

In 1976, the American mystery writer was penning a book called *Bank Robber*, and he decided that he needed to know what it would be like to rob a bank. So he decided to give it a try.

First of all, he sent a copy of his manuscript to his daughter, and warned her that what he was about to do in the name of research might get him into trouble. He wasn't wrong. When he entered his chosen bank, fully intending to rob it, Drummond had barely had time to produce his pistol before a security guard, quick on the draw, shot him dead in an instant.

Coining it

The Grand Canyon in Arizona is perhaps the world's largest wishing-well, with countless visitors throwing in coins and making wishes from the numerous handy overlooks here and there, the more treacherous of which have fences to prevent people from falling to their deaths.

Some coins would would fall to the valley floor, where the wish-maker intended, but others would pile up on the surfaces of small towering plateaux below the overlooks, which made lucrative pickings for anyone stupid enough to risk life and limb to collect them. And so it was in March 2000 that one chap with an eye for a quick buck decided he'd make the most of the riches on offer, after jumping over one of the wooden safety barriers and spying the money below.

He stuffed as many coins as he could into a bag, and then tried to jump back and grab the fence. The weight of the bag pulled him back, however, and down he went, coins and all, to the depths of the unforgiving canyon.

Full of holes

In 2004 workers in a funeral parlour in Latvia must have thought they'd got the victim of the *Psycho* shower scene on the slab – except that it belonged to an eighty-seven-year-old man. His body was virtually perforated, and yet a doctor who had visited the victim's home in Riga had failed to notice that he had been stabbed forty-five times, and came to he conclusion the elderly gentleman had died from natural causes.

The victim's wife had called the doctor initially, but had been too shocked to reveal what had really happened. Because of the man's advanced age, the doctor appeared not to have given him a proper examination, having decided that he'd had a long life which had reached its natural end.

Police weren't as slow-witted, however, and launched an immediate murder investigation. A neighbour was eventually taken in for questioning in connection with the highly suspicious death.

Bent the rules

Not only did an unfortunate thirty-year-old man from the Bronx in New York hold a gun without a licence, but he had a tendency to keep it in his waistband, which would ultimately lead to fatal consequences.

In September 2002, the guy was adjusting the illegal .380 Beretta while sitting in his car with his girlfriend in a car park at 3.30 one morning, when he accidentally shot himself in his upper leg. He had made the mistake of hitting an artery, and was pronounced dead some time later.

Hot car

Not all thieves are inconsiderate. One twenty-eight-year-old car robber reasoned that the vehicles he stole would earn their owners insurance money far more quickly if he burned them when he'd finished with them, instead of just abandoning them.

But in March 1998, the crook met his end in a van that he'd filched from Pittsburgh, Pennsylvania, which turned out to be the hottest vehicle of his car-thieving career. What he hadn't realized when he'd got in and slammed the door was that the lock on the inside of the driver's door didn't work properly. After setting fire to the vehicle from the inside, as was his practice, he found that he couldn't get out. His burned body was later found in the van's smouldering wreckage.

In the soup

Shoichi Murakami was a notorious gang leader from Tokyo, active during the mid to late twentieth century, who would live (or perhaps die) to become – literally – a part of the community in which he lived.

Murakami had been involved in a protracted and deadly gang war until, one day, five hatchet-wielding gentlemen arrived at his restaurant and killed him, before chopping him up into many pieces. They managed to hide the largest parts of him in various refuse containers around the restaurant, but in order to destroy identifying features such as fingerprints, his hands were duly cooked and made into a meat-and-noodle soup, which was consumed by more than fifty blissfully ignorant customers.

Rapid end

How do you smuggle something as unwieldy as elk antlers out of Yellowstone Park? How not to do it would be to use a rubber dinghy, but this was the getaway method chosen by two locals who wanted to leave the park with some shed antlers in 1985. The antlers could have been worth about $7 a pound, and as a large set can weigh up to 30 pounds the two men could have made quite a killing.

The problem was that it was illegal to take the antlers, and it wouldn't be easy to get away with them without being seen. There were ranger checkpoints on the roads, so a car was out of the question, and they certainly couldn't carry them in backpacks. Eventually they decided on a boat, or more specifically a rubber raft. They decided to smuggle the antlers out at night along the Gardiner River, which runs out of the park and through the town of Gardiner, Montana.

Antlers, as everyone knows, are pointed; the 'boat' was made of inflated rubber; the men were not very bright – three factors that were bound to lead to tragedy, which they did.

The river had some rapids, and during the precarious voyage one of the bouncing antlers punctured the dinghy, leaving the men to swim – against the current. One fellow got to the shore and managed to hitch a ride into town. The other was not so lucky, and his corpse was found on a beach a week later.

Teething problems

The *Johannesburg Citizen* of 16 May 1991 tells the story of a fifty-six-year-old conman who posed as a sewing-machine technician to trick his way into a house in Alicante, Spain. He managed to make off with the equivalent of £80, but the woman of the house chased him and he tripped, inadvertently swallowing his dentures. He choked to death.

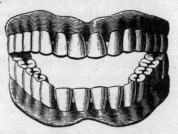

Swallowing false teeth is not as rare an occurrence as we might think. In September 1992 it also happened to twenty-four-year-old Abdul Fadli Talib, an off-duty bus conductor, who fell asleep on the back seat of a bus from Kuala Lumpur to Seremban in western Malaysia. He, too, swallowed his dentures and choked to death.

There for the asking

A thirty-four-year-old Sydney man took a fancy to the engine of an old Bedford tip-truck in September 1990, so he decided to nick it. However, whereas most people would take out an engine from the top, using a block and tackle or other lifting device, our man decided to take it from the bottom, with disastrous consequences.

The truck was parked outside a glass-recycling company's premises in Alexandria when the would-be thief got to work. He decided to remove the engine – which would usually take three or four men to lift –

from beneath the truck. Under the cab he went, and began loosening the bolts that held the engine in place. Then came the crash, as the engine block broke free and landed on his face. Death was instant.

After the body was discovered the next morning, the manager of the company revealed that the truck was about to be scrapped. 'If he'd come and asked me for it, I would have given it to him,' he said.

Police believed that the thief had at least one accomplice, judging by the pool of vomit they found at the scene of the attempted crime.

Curse of the flying fruit and veg

In July 1989, while shopping in east London, a fifty-six-year-old man was fatally injured by a flying turnip – and he wasn't the only person to have been hit by airborn fruits and vegetables during the same period, according to police. His death was treated as murder after he was

hit by a turnip hurled from a passing car. The impact caused him to suffer a ruptured spleen, as well as chronic pulmonary disease and acute respiratory failure.

Detective Superintendent Graham Howard said police were investigating a number of incidents in the area in which items of fruit and veg had been thrown from vehicles, including a jogger who had been hit by a cabbage in April that year.

Death by Dining

Food generally sustains us, but sometimes it can kill us – whether it be the food itself or the circumstances connected with food and its consumption.

Starvation diet

This is not so much death by dining as death by not dining.

For nowhere does 'out of the frying pan' hold true more than in the case of Charles VII of France, who died in 1461. He was convinced that he would be poisoned by his own son, and, understandably, he didn't want to die. But in avoiding the consumption of food for fear of being poisoned, he killed himself through starvation.

Condiment killing

Some superstitions are not to be taken with a pinch of salt, it would seem.

Nicholas Augustus de la Baume was a seventeenth-century soldier who had proved himself as fearless and gallant in battle. But he was also superstitious – so much so that he died in absolute terror when salt from a salt shaker was accidentally thrown over him.

Cardinal sin

The moral of this tale is that if you plan to poison someone, keep your eyes open.

A sixteenth-century Florentine noblewoman called Bianca Capello failed to do just that when she tried to poison Cardinal Ferdinand with a tart she had prepared specifically for the occasion, but while Bianca was distracted, the canny cardinal switched his tart for hers.

Hard to digest

What makes Private Harry Flynn's death so stupid is its very mundaneness. In 1917 he had the dubious distinction of being America's first casualty of the First World War, yet he died of indigestion.

After he'd been conscripted into the army, he carried out basic training at Camp Upton at Yaphank on Long Island. But he didn't even complete the course before the fatal indigestion fit took hold and caused his sudden death. However, he was still buried with full military honours, complete with bugle-playing and all the other frills and trappings associated with such occasions in the US.

Bon appétit

Lord Astor (1848–1919) loved his food. This American-born British journalist and financier – great-grandson of John Jacob Astor, whose name is given to the Astor Library in New York City – was both gourmet and gourmand, it seems, and was used to stuffing himself with huge amounts of grub on a regular basis, beginning each day with a breakfast of prawns and artichokes. He would usually arrange his gastronomic gorging a month in advance, giving his chef orders accordingly.

In early October 1919 Astor requested a future meal that would include pheasant, fried oyster and several other high-quality culinary goodies, but he was fated never to sample these delights: halfway through the month he downed a surfeit of roast mutton and macaroni with a bucket of Beaune wine.

He overate and subsequently died.

Deaths in History

The phenomenon of the 'stupid death' isn't specific to modern times. On the contrary, there have been numerous occasions throughout history where unfortunate individuals have met their maker in less than ordinary ways; some in stranger circumstances than others.

Death of a princess

When the Native American chief's daughter Pocahontas (c.1595–1617) travelled to the Old World in the early seventeenth century, it was ostensibly to be exposed to its charms. Instead, she was exposed to something that brought about her premature death.

Pocahontas – whose name means 'playful one' – married a Virginian settler called John Rolfe in 1614, and two years later travelled to England with their young son Thomas.

But in 1617 it was Old World disease to which the Native American princess fell victim – tuberculosis, and possibly pneumonia. What no one had realized was that her immune system wasn't 'aware' of such illnesses, and the party managed to travel only 20 miles (32 kilometres) down the Thames before she became ill and had to be taken ashore for urgent treatment.

Pocahontas died three weeks later aged just twenty-two.

A point made . . . at a cost

The nobility of the fifth-century monk Telemachus might have looked stupid on the surface, but his extreme personal sacrifice turned out not to be wholly in vain.

According to the writings of Theodoret, Bishop of Cyrus, in 404 CE the brave monk leaped into the centre of the Colosseum in protest at the gladiatorial 'entertainment' on offer. Though most of the more barbaric Roman 'sports' had ceased by this time, Telemachus still wanted to register his opposition, and so when the show was about to begin, he rushed down from the crowd to the middle of the arena and stood between two hulking gladiators, shouting, 'In the name of Christ, stop!' While the crowd laughed at his feeble efforts, one of the gladiators first hit him to the ground, and then dealt him a fatal blow to the stomach. The monk later died on the amphitheatre floor.

Though Telemachus had had to pay for his beliefs with his life, his efforts were rewarded posthumously, however, when three days later Emperor Honorius responded to the monk's selfless campaign by closing down all the arenas.

Dead Fred

Holy Roman Emperor Frederick I (1122–90) instigated the third Crusade to recapture the Holy Land in 1189. The following year, he handed over the government of the empire to his son Henry, and set off for Asia Minor.

He and his men trudged for days across dry summer desert, and on 10 June 1190, feeling somewhat parched, he threw himself into the Calycadnus river in Cilicia (now the Göksu river in Turkey) for a welcome bathe. Unfortunately for Fred, he sank and drowned.

His son was crowned Holy Roman Emperor Henry VI a year later.

Deadly perfume

According to some sources, when the French royal family secretly fled from Paris during the Revolution, the reason they were discovered was because they had been recognized at Varennes while changing horses. However, one tenacious tale reveals that it was Marie Antoinette's perfume that gave them away.

Though Marie Antoinette and her husband King Louis XVI were disguised as commoners, when she emerged from their carriage at Varennes in 1791, her fragrance revealed that she was far from being a mere *citoyenne*.

Forced to return to Paris by local republicans, they were to remain in the city until their eventual executions in 1793.

Mahomet's mountain of love

'Yet each man kills the thing he loves,' wrote Oscar Wilde in *The Ballad of Reading Gaol*, the lengthy poem he penned after his release from prison. Perhaps the Turkish Emperor Mahomet I had crossed Wilde's mind; a man who really had the hots for a beautiful Greek girl called Irene, whom he stupidly killed in 1415.

Mahomet had been spending a lot of time with the girl, to the chagrin of his counsellors, who thought she had too much influence over their leader's conduct. Feeling somewhat resentful of their overbearing concern, Mahomet summoned them all together, after dressing his true-love in the finest of clothes. Then he paraded her before the team of counsellors, to show them just what a drop-dead-gorgeous dish she was. They conceded that she really was quite something, and they apologized for criticizing their emperor's choice of concubine.

Then, rather unexpectedly, came Irene's violent demise, as Mahomet pulled her towards him by the hair, bent back her head, and sliced it off at the neck with his sword.

That would teach them to disapprove of his favoured paramour. Duh!

Hanging about

It was not unusual to see people pilloried (held in stocks publicly) in Britain in the eighteenth century, as it was a popular form of punishment. So it would therefore have made sense for those in charge of this apparatus to make arrangements to accommodate all shapes and sizes of miscreant likely to be paying them a visit.

In the case of Thomas Todd, however, they failed him badly and let him down in more ways than one. Todd was quite short, and consequently his feet didn't touch the ground, so when his head was put through the hole, without any support below, he simply hung there.

By the time officials managed to reach him, it was too late, and Todd had ceased to be.

Jumbo boast

General John Sedgwick is probably better off for not knowing what was said of him after he uttered eight of the most stupid last words in history.

It was during the American Civil War, while the Union general was at the Battle of Spotsylvania in 1864.

'They couldn't hit an elephant at this distance,' he said of the enemy, with great – if misplaced – bravado. Well, he was right: they couldn't hit an elephant because there wasn't one around. However, the opposing troops did hit General John Sedgwick. Fatally.

Death by mattress

Though French commander Admiral Decres had survived the blast that had destroyed his ship during the Battle of Aboukir in 1799, he ended up dying on his own mattress – when it exploded.

It's not known exactly who was responsible for this naval officer's untimely end, but someone – possibly a servant – had laid a trail of gunpowder to the mattress and set it alight with fatal consequences.

La fin

Many have died for their art – even chefs. The famous seventeenth-century French chef Vatel did just that after he had been asked to prepare a dinner at Chantilly in honour of Louis XIV, the 'Sun King'.

Vatel (1622–76) ordered a large quantity of fish from nearby ports, but his supplier told him he couldn't honour the full order, and delivered only two small boxes. When Vatel demanded, 'Is that all there is?' the fishmonger replied, 'Yes,' meaning only that there would be no more fish that day from his own fleet. But Vatel took it to mean no fish, full stop.

This led Vatel to come to a full stop of his own, because after crying out, 'I cannot endure this disgrace!' he retired to his chamber, trapped his sword in his door with the point towards him, and threw himself on it.

Death by beard

If there had been a book of *Guinness World Records* in the sixteenth century, Hans Steininger would have had an entry for having the world's longest beard. He might also have got a mention for being stupid enough to let his oversized facial hair be the unlikely cause of his death.

Steininger was an Austrian burgher in 1567 when he met his demise while climbing a flight of steps leading to the council chamber in the town of Brunn. Unfortunately, he trod on his beard and tripped, tumbling down the stone stairs, causing severe head injuries, from which he eventually died.

Holy gunshots, Batman!

Maurice James Butler's epitaph says it all, really:

> Sacred To The Memory Of
> Captain Maurice James Butler,
> Royal Irish Rifles,
> Accidentally Shot Dead By His
> Batman On The Fourth Day Of
> April, 1882
> 'Well Done, Thou Good And
> Faithful Servant'

The hair (or lack of it) and the tortoise

Aeschylus (525–456 BCE), was the father of Greek tragedy, but even he couldn't have anticipated the kind of misfortune that the fates had in store for him.

As well as a great tragedian – the earliest of Athens's great tragic poets and the predecessor of Sophocles and Euripides – Aeschylus was a soldier, and had fought successfully against the Persians at Marathon in 490 BCE and at Salamís in 480 BCE, but it wasn't as a fighting man that he met his end. According to Pliny, it was as the unexpected recipient of an airborn tortoise, which fell from the sky on to his head.

It was believed that the reptile had been taken aloft by an eagle, as eagles would often seize the creatures from the ground, carry them up into the air and drop them down onto rocks to crack open their shells. Now Aeschylus had a bald head, and a hairless pate can easily be mistaken for . . . well, you've probably got the picture.

In his great play *Agamemnon*, he wrote, 'Hold him alone truly fortunate who has ended his life in happy wellbeing.' One wonders whether Aeschylus would agree that death by tortoise amounts to dying in a jolly state. There must be worse ways to go, so perhaps he was indeed 'truly fortunate'.

Incidentally, history doesn't tell us whether the tortoise survived its double misfortune.

Duelling bozos

It was the American naval officer Stephen Decatur (1779–1820) who first uttered the famous phrase 'our country, right or wrong', in a toast. But after finding himself embroiled in a duel with a fellow officer, he managed to die in a rather bizarre way.

The man who challenged him to the contest on 22 March 1820 was a disgraced navy captain called James Barren, in whose court martial Decatur had been involved.

Unusually, because his opponent was very nearsighted, Decatur, the skilled duellist, agreed to an unusual change in the rules: they would exchange shots from a distance of just eight paces.

As a reward for his misplaced courtesy, he was shot by Barren, and died.

That bloody nose!

When you've conquered just about the whole of Asia, you expect to die of something a little less wussy than a nosebleed. But this is what happened to the notorious Attila the Hun (c.406–453 CE), who had pillaged and plundered, looted and laid waste to untold numbers of villages in his role as warrior extraordinaire.

Not only was his death his own stupid fault, but he also left a disappointed bride all alone on her wedding night.

Attila married the young Ildico in 453, and so taken was he with her, apparently, that he stuffed himself silly on his wedding night, which was odd, for despite his reputation, he would usually drink and eat sparingly during large banquets.

It would seem that in a bout of overexuberance, he consumed far too much food and drink, and during the night suffered such a massive nosebleed that he drowned in his own blood, too drunk to notice. His bride was too frightened to call anyone and Attila's attendants were reluctant to enter his chamber lest they disturbed their master and his new wife the morning after their wedding celebrations.

The mighty Attila was found dead the following day.

Major error . . .

Americans might be whistling 'Dixie' now instead of saluting the Star-Spangled Banner if it hadn't been for Major John Barry.

Barry was commanding a detachment of Confederate troops on 2 May 1863, in Chancellorsville (now Chancellor), near Fredericksburg, Virginia, when he saw what he thought were some mounted Union officers and so he ordered his men to fire on them. Unfortunately, one of the officers was his own boss, General Thomas Jonathan 'Stonewall' Jackson (1824–63), widely regarded as the South's best military leader, but for whose demise the South might have won the Civil War. Jackson was hit three times and lost his left arm, and as a consequence of the trauma and loss of blood he grew weak, and died on 10 May.

Hello, Mum!

The Greek tragedian Euripides (480–406 BCE) tells the story of Pentheus, King of Thebes, who opposed the practice of worshipping Dionysus, the god of wine. It is said that one day he climbed a tree to watch a group of Bacchic women cavorting. He hoped he wouldn't be seen, but he was eventually spotted by the women and, in their frenzy, they tore him to bits.

What makes it rather stupid is that his dear old mum was among them, but according to the story in Euripides's *Bacchae*, she was so out of her mind in Bacchic fervour that she mistook him for a beast.

Bye, Mum!

Domestic violence takes on a whole new dimension in the case of the Roman Emperor Nero (37–68 CE). Not only did he have his mother killed for her criticism of his mistress, but he proceeded to murder said mistress once she had become his wife. She was Poppaea Sabina, and was Nero's second wife, after he had divorced (and later executed) Octavia, his first.

But Nero – the man accused of fiddling while Rome burned – was known for his tantrums, and, during the course of a particularly nasty disagreement, kicked her in the stomach, killing her. How careless!

Third time unlucky

The noted French explorer René-Robert Cavelier, Sieur de la Salle (1643–87) couldn't have got himself into a greater muddle if he'd tried.

He had set out to explore North America, travelled on the Mississippi to the Gulf of Mexico (and claimed the entire valley for France), and journeyed all the way back along the Mississippi and on to Quebec. Then he sailed home for refinancing before returning to North America by sea.

But this time it was not plain sailing. He mistakenly landed on the Texas coast instead of in the Mississippi delta, and then walked thousands of miles with his men looking for the Mississippi, before sailing for Canada. But he got lost in stormy seas and found himself back in the Gulf of Mexico.

A tenacious character, however, he tried again, and again. By the third unsuccessful attempt his men had had enough. Understandably fed up with the situation, they bumped him off.

Do It Yourself

For so many people, the Grim Reaper doesn't need to creep up on them, because they've sent him an invitation. DIY deaths abound. Whether by suicides or just unfortunate or bizarre circumstances, people find ingenious ways of bringing about their own demise.

Tie-die

Francis Ellis was great with knots, and he loved to demonstrate how easily he could tie himself up in them. One day, in 1931, this young Cambridge student set about the ultimate in self-bondage, and was found dead in his room with his wrists tied behind his back and his face in a cushion. But that was not all: his legs were tied, and so was most of his body. Handkerchiefs, cloths, webbing and straps had been utilized in whatever way possible to add to the bindings; he was also gagged.

Police at first suspected murder or manslaughter, but the forensic pathologist, Sir Bernard Spilsbury, succeeded in demonstrating how Ellis had been able to do it all to himself.

Spilsbury showed that Ellis had bound himself in this way while standing and had put cushions on the floor to break his fall (as his legs were tied, too, of course). But he had probably stunned himself on hitting the floor, and had remained stunned long enough to suffocate, having fallen face first into a cushion.

Up, up – and away

Being the widow of the great aeronaut François Blanchard, Madame Blanchard really ought to have known better than to risk the combination of a hot-air balloon and fireworks. But she did just that. And it killed her.

Her husband François (1753–1809), also known as Jean-Pierre Blanchard, had crossed the English Channel from Dover to Calais in 1785 with John Jeffries, an American doctor. In the same year he also gave the first successful demonstration of the use of a parachute.

It was while his widow was doing a balloon ascent over Paris in 1819 that she let off fireworks she had brought with her to celebrate the ascent. It's not difficult to imagine what happened: one firework hit the balloon, setting fire to it and causing balloon, basket and Mme Blanchard to fall from a great height.

Breaking the ice

Sometimes, ice can be so thick that it's possible to drive vehicles on it, but it certainly wasn't recommended by the US Coastguard when David Manley decided to attempt such a feat in March 2003 in Michigan.

The forty-one-year-old even had a physical warning, because, as he drove his pick-up on to the icy surface of Saginaw Bay on a chilly morning, it sank – but on this occasion he managed to escape by reaching the shore, albeit cold and wet.

When you're determined to be really stupid, though, it would seem that no warning can succeed. This guy was so determined to drive on the ice that the next time he had a go it was during a day of sunshine and warm temperatures.

He returned to the ice and drove an all-terrain vehicle on to it. Inevitably, down it went, and Manley made his manly exit from this world by sinking below the ice for the very last time.

Fast food, fast death

According to the newspaper *Hoy de La Paz*, twenty-one-year-old security guard Victor Alba was trying to 'impress some female friends', when he placed the barrel of his .38 revolver at his head at a fast-food joint at La Paz, Mexico, in December 1997.

It can only be assumed he thought that all the cylinder's chambers were empty when he pulled the stunt, because he pulled the trigger, too, and died instantly.

Calling a Holt

To this day an air of mystery still surrounds the death of the Australian Prime Minister, Harold Holt, in December 1967.

As the country's top politician, he was usually surrounded by bodyguards and flunkies, and so it was inconceivable that Holt, an accomplished swimmer and skin diver, had been able to walk to a near-deserted beach in Portsea, Victoria, and simply disappear.

Being a prominent death, a number of theories have been suggested, including one to the effect that it was his support for the Vietnam War that led to his assassination. But it's more likely that on the day he died the ocean's powerful currents were too much for him.

His body was never found.

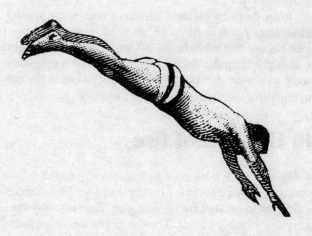

Game set his match

Computers can be addictive – especially when playing games on them. In fact, it's possible to become so stupid about them that you'll sit in front of a screen for hours with no notion of the passing of time.

A thirty-one-year-old addict collapsed and died in 2004 after spending twenty hours playing a game called *Saga* in an Internet café, according to the *South China Morning Post*. An employee of the café was quoted as saying that the addict would often play for more than ten hours per day.

Hair-raising!

A fifty-three-year-old French shop manager called Claude Jules was rather vain, and, when he bought a £750 toupee in 1992, he was eager to try it on immediately.

After daubing the said hairpiece with some special glue, Jules put it in place on his head as soon as he got into his car. But what he didn't know was that the glue was highly flammable, and the fumes that it released were so strong that they ignited, which caused the car to explode, and Jules was killed instantly.

In the line of fire

Being shot with your own gun may look stupid enough, but in 1928 one Mr A. V. Bonham of Arkansas managed to be shot by his *own* gun. That is to say the gun shot him – by itself. The circumstances were these.

Bonham had arrived home to find that his son had been playing with petrol and matches, and had set the house on fire. So Bonham and his neighbours salvaged what they could from the burning building, and when they had managed to save as much as they could, Bonham could do no more than stand and watch the flames continue to consume his home.

But then there was a bang. A neighbour, Mack Medley, felt something brush the peak of his cap, and then saw Bonham drop to the ground, shouting, 'I'm shot!'

He got up and staggered a little, and then hit the ground again, dead.

The love affair that most Americans have with firearms meant that Mr Bonham had kept a revolver in the drawer of his bureau. As the flames licked at the bureau, the loaded gun grew hotter and hotter, until eventually, it went off – and who should be standing in the line of fire but poor ill-fated Mr Bonham.

Automatic death

We all know the principles of Russian roulette: one bullet in one chamber of the randomly spun cylinder of a revolver, with no one knowing at which cocking it will be moved into the breech.

But at an impromptu game of Russian roulette in Texas in 2000, a Houston man decided to do it with a .45 semi-automatic. He didn't realize, it would seem, that this kind of pistol automatically inserts a round into the firing chamber when the gun is cocked.

He lost the game, of course – and his life.

I'm dead, so I'll kill myself

Hearing word of your own death can be quite upsetting, as Mark Twain discovered when he read his own obituary and was reported in the *New York Journal* of 1 June 1897 as saying, 'The report of my death was an exaggeration.' (This is often misquoted, incidentally, as 'Reports of my death have been greatly exaggerated.')

Armando Cassa, a twenty-four-year-old Puerto Rican, became far more upset than that, though, when he heard reports that he had apparently died in a fire. His reaction was far more dramatic, if less witty, than that of Twain.

So distressed was he, in fact, that he jumped from a high-rise flat and killed himself.

Don't hang about

In 1976, one Mr D. H. Beenan of New Zealand was so horrified by the fact that hanging was still in force in his country that he decided to demonstrate just how barbaric a form of punishment it was.

In front of an audience that included his own fiancée, Bebe Trumper, Mr Beenan slipped the noose around his neck. Just as Bebe remarked on 'how horrible the whole thing is,' her fiancé jumped from the chair and choked himself to death.

Whether this was a dramatic and elaborate manner of committing suicide, it isn't certain. Perhaps he thought he would survive to tell the tale. For whatever reason though, it wasn't very clever.

Cool!

Dmitry Butakov could almost be excused for thinking himself immortal after surviving a 10,000-volt electric shock in 1992.

So deluded was he by this mistaken belief that, some years later, the forty-two-year-old invited journalists to his city of Lipetsk in central European Russia to watch him drink some antifreeze. Immortality obviously wasn't on the agenda, as Butakov collapsed into a coma and eventually died.

In hot water

A soak in a hot tub was just the thing at the end of a day doing nothing much at all. Wesley and Helen Laroya of Simi Valley, California, had joined the hot-tub craze back in 1979 and had one installed in their back yard.

One night in May 1979 they decided to take a dip in their hot tub, and despite the fact that the couple both suffered from high blood pressure, they turned up the thermostat to 110°F (38°C). Unfortunately for both Laroyas, they fell sound asleep – and didn't wake up.

Both had been drinking heavily, and a combination of the water temperature, the booze and their own high blood pressure ensured they succumbed to hypothermia, alcohol poisoning and heart disease.

Crackers!

In January 2002, police in Croatia reported that a man had blown himself up while trying to chainsaw his way into a hand grenade.

Quite why he had such an incendiary device in his possession remains open to conjecture, but it was believed that he was trying to get at the explosive inside in order to make some fireworks for the New Year holiday.

Not an all-right jack

In 2003 a New Zealander called Phil jacked up his car in order to do some repairs, but the jack didn't elevate the vehicle high enough. After scratching his head, Phil removed the car's battery and placed the jack on top of it, which gave him plenty of room to work.

The trouble was, even the most robust of car batteries is not made to withstand the weight of a jack and part of a car. Not surprisingly it collapsed, toppling the jack and dropping the car on top of hapless Phil, trapping him fast. Bearing such a weight on his chest severely restricted his breathing, and so it wasn't long before Phil had breathed his last.

What makes this death even more stupid is that Phil had been employed as an accident-prevention officer at a big food-processing plant. And ten years before his death he'd been working under a car and suffered a similar jack collapse, but that time had only broken one of his legs. Some people never learn . . .

Oh, crumbs!

The seventeenth-century English playwright Tomas Otway (1652–85) was just thirty-three when he died in penury.

The author of plays such as *Alcibiades* (1675) and *Don Carlos* (1676), in spite of this success, he died in poverty, and it was after he had begged for food – and had been given a loaf of bread – that he desperately gulped at it and choked to death.

Air head

A farmer in São Paulo needed to remove a beehive from an orange tree in September 2002. So, bearing in mind that bees sting, especially when they're angry, he decided to burn the hive, but in order to protect his face he covered his head with a plastic bag, which he sealed tightly at the neck. Taking a torch, he went off to engage in a bit of arson.

After something of a lengthy absence, his wife grew worried and went off in search of her errant husband. When she eventually found him, he was dead.

His death wasn't a result of anaphylactic shock caused by an allergic reaction to bee venom, as one might suspect, but was simply due to a lack of oxygen. He hadn't put any ventilation holes in the plastic bag to enable him to breathe.

Please speak after the bang

Quite how you could mistake a Smith & Wesson .38 Special revolver for a telephone is anybody's guess, but forty-seven-year-old Ken Charles Barger managed it in 1991.

According to the *Hickory Daily Record*, Barger, of Newton in North Carolina, woke to the sound of his ringing bedside telephone. But another little item he kept by his bed was the .38 revolver, which he accidentally fired when he drew it to his ear.

One, toe, three, four . . .

Jean-Baptiste Lully (1633–87) was a favourite at the court of Louis XIV. This Italian-born French composer had entered the king's service as a ballet dancer and a violinist, becoming music master to the royal family in 1662, and later helped to establish opera in France. He was also the composer of, among other things, the ballet *Alcidiane* (1658), and collaborated with none other than Molière on a series of comedy ballets.

As well as composing pieces of music, he also conducted orchestras, and it was while engaged in this particular musical activity that Lully sustained an unfortunate injury. In the seventeenth century it was customary to bash a heavy baton on the floor while conducting, to help the orchestra to keep time. This is what Lully was doing when he struck his toe on one of the downward strokes. The painful blow caused a severe bout of blood poisoning, which eventually killed him.

On the lighter side

When you want to check the barrel of a muzzleloader, what's the best way to shed a little light on the matter? Well, a cigarette lighter, of course!

Though it's clearly a stupid thing to do, this is what a man from Jay County, Indiana, did when the weapon discharged in his face, killing him, according to the *Indianapolis Star* of 4 December 1996.

The incident occurred at 11.30 one night. Investigators said the man was cleaning a .54-calibre muzzleloader that hadn't been firing as it should. When he ignited the lighter, and the lighter ignited the gunpowder, the subsequent explosion ignited his head – with a bang.

The wait is killing me

John Buckley just couldn't wait a day longer for the police to arrest him and throw him into jail. In fact, the strain took its toll to such an extent that he ended up paying with his life.

After pleading guilty to drunken driving, forty-seven-year-old Buckley, of Brisbane, Australia, was sentenced to two months in prison in 1974, fined AUS$250 and banned from driving for two years. However, there was a mix-up in the courts, and, although he had been sentenced, no warrant was ever issued for his actual arrest. He kept a bag packed for three years with a few necessities such as nightwear and toothbrush, expecting that knock on the door. But it never came.

Unlikely though it may sound, Buckley was so worried by his impending arrest that he finally cracked – and shot himself.

An ill-starred demise

Did he predict his own death or didn't he? We'll leave you to decide for yourself whether Gerolamo Cardano (1501–76), the Italian gambler, astrologer, doctor and mathematician – and sometime charlatan – had foresight regarding the day he was due to pass over into the next world.

Not only did Cardano treat the Archbishop of St Andrews in Scotland for an asthmatic problem, but he also cast the horoscope of King Edward the VI of England. He even had the audacity to cast a horoscope for Jesus Christ, and was arrested by the Inquisition, but he recanted and eventually enjoyed a pension granted by Pope Pius V.

Though some say this is fancy, he is best known for drawing up an astrological prediction of the exact hour of his own death. He calculated it would take place on 21 September 1576, which indeed it did, but not as you might expect.

When the day came, Cardano was rather disappointed to find that he was in the rudest of health, and the fact that he had now been proved wrong meant that his career as a predictor of the future was uncertain. So distressed was he by this worrying thought that he promptly killed himself.

Consequently, his prediction came true – in a way.

Not looking down in the mouth

Horace Wells fell in love with the tools of his trade to the point of addiction. Literally. And it led to his suicide in prison.

Wells (1815–48) was the American dentist who discovered that laughing gas – or nitrous oxide – could be used as an anaesthetic. He had been watching a travelling show when he noticed that the gas induced anaesthesia, which led him to try it on himself and on patients during tooth extractions.

Eventually, he gave up dentistry and became a travelling salesman. He went to Paris to set himself up as an expert on nitrous oxide, but on his arrival he found that the gas had been superseded by chloroform and ether, and so he had no choice but to return to New York.

It was at this time that he began experimenting on himself with a number of different anaesthetics – and became addicted. On one occasion he got rather high on a particular chemical, and ended up spraying two women with sulphuric acid. In prison he wrote a letter blaming chloroform for his problems.

However, his stupidity gave him the ultimate get-out-of-jail card: he anaesthetized himself with some chloroform and slashed his thigh with a razor, which caused him to bleed to death.

Sharp practice

UN police in East Timor (now Timor-Leste) thought the young man they had found in a pool of mud and blood had been the victim of a street crime in the capital, Dili. But this wasn't so.

The unfortunate fellow had been in the habit of carrying his two long knives – which he used as weapons – down the waistband of his trousers, completely oblivious of what this might do to his delicate bits.

So, when the man hopped over a fence, landed in a large puddle of mud and slipped, it was the femoral artery that suffered most damage. As he tumbled, one of the knives punctured the artery, causing rapid loss of blood. He had bled to death before staggering even ten feet from the puddle.

Oh, pants!

Human ingenuity has devised all kinds of things to keep people happy in the bedroom: sensuous lingerie, things that vibrate, the paraphernalia of bondage and S&M. Perhaps one of the most innovative is edible knickers, which can, presumably, be nibbled at until there is nothing left of the original item of clothing.

But it didn't quite work that way for forty-four-year-old Jean-Louis Toubon in Marseilles in May 2003. He was consuming his girlfriend's knickers when part of the garment got stuck in his throat, and he choked to death.

A tale with bite

As you would expect of the founder of the best-known detective agency in the world, Allan Pinkerton had a life of some adventure.

Born in Scotland in 1819, he went to live near Chicago in 1842 and became a barrel maker. One day he caught a gang of counterfeiters and was duly elected county sheriff.

It was in 1850 that he formed Pinkerton's National Detective Agency, and, among other things, he organized scab labour to stand in for strikers. Judging by the title of his 1878 book *Strikers, Communists and Tramps*, he didn't much like men who went on strike.

One morning in 1884, however, Pinkerton's life of adventure took an unfortunate turn when he slipped while out walking, and bit his tongue as he fell. The injured member became gangrenous, and eventually led to his death.

Stretching a point

In the early part of the nineteenth century, one Peter Harkan was a demonstrator for surgeon Phillip Crampton at Dublin's Meath Hospital. The school of anatomy there, of which Crampton was director, often made use of bodies supplied by grave robbers.

One night when Harkan was engaged in a bit of body snatching, he was caught by a watchman as he tried to escape over a cemetery wall. He had been accompanied by a group of students, however, and, after the watchman had grabbed his legs, the students took firm hold of his arms to try to help him escape. A veritable tug-o'-war ensued.

It would seem that the watchman must have been a

powerful chap, because, despite being outnumbered by the band of students, he held on like a terrier. The result was that poor Peter Harkan was stretched to death as if he'd been on the rack in a dungeon, and he died of internal injuries.

That's all, folks!

Remember those cartoon capers in which Bugs Bunny or some other cartoon character is sawing a tree branch on the wrong side from where he's sitting? It's that sort of stupidity that must have motivated the chap who entered a hot cavern in Chihuahua, Mexico, in 2001.

There are two such caverns in the area, both about 1,200 feet (365 metres) below the earth's surface, and both containing clear selenite crystals that measure over 20 feet (6 metres) long. At the time of this incident, they had not been long discovered. Selenite is a transparent, colourless gypsum, which holds together in such a way as to reveal lustrous crystal faces, and entire stalactites of this beautiful crystal hang from the cavern ceilings – very attractive trophies if you can get one out and get it home.

The man who hacked away at a beautiful selenite stalactite in 2001 could well have been a hapless cartoon character, because he decided to stand right under the thing as he chopped. The inevitable happened, and down came the stalactite, pinning him to the ground. Alone, and without any means of escape, he roasted in the cavern's 108°F (42°C) heat.

Alarming incident

Forgetting to switch off your burglar alarm on entering your premises can at most be an embarrassment and an annoyance to neighbours, and might even alert the police if your security installation has a direct link to the local nick.

Such a nuisance can be avoided (at a price), if you decide to use a rather unusual form of security, as Giacario Burranti did in his Milan shop in November 1992.

After he'd been burgled ten times, Burranti booby-trapped the premises with a bomb, in an effort to prevent any further crimes from taking place on his property. The problem was that he forgot to switch it off when he entered the building, and was duly blown to bits.

Watch me while I shoot myself (1)

Showing off your prized acquisitions can be fatal – especially if they're firearms – but that's what happened to one Anthony J. Drexel III, the young scion of a rich and successful New York business family, in 1893.

Drexel took some guests to his pride and joy – his gun room. Picking up a favoured exhibit – a pistol – he said, 'Here's one you haven't seen before.' But in waving it about he accidentally pulled the trigger and shot himself dead.

It could have been worse – at least all the guests survived.

Watch me while I shoot myself (2)

Waving guns about is always best avoided, as this second tale of woe illustrates. Terry Kath was a member of the rock band Chicago, and had a passion for firearms. One day in 1978 he was showing off a new revolver in front of the rest of the band in Los Angeles, and began a pretend game of Russian roulette, thinking the chamber was empty.

It wasn't.

'Don't worry, this thing's not loaded,' he said.

It was.

The .45 bullet penetrated Kath's brain, shattering it. The irony is that Chicago's manager had told reporters only recently – after rumours of Kath's departure from the band – that the only way he would leave 'is in a pine box', which is just what he did.

Kath was only thirty-two when he died; the Los Angeles coroner ruled that there had been an 'accidental gunshot wound to the head under the influence of alcohol and drugs'.

Slash with a flash

Most of us have crossed our legs tightly from time to time, just bursting for a pee, and wishing we'd been before leaving the house. Of course it's easier for men, who can simply look for a tree or a hedge to nip behind and protect their modesty.

That's probably what Australian Sammy Bungan found himself doing one day during the last century – but maybe there weren't any trees or hedges located conveniently in the outback, because he chose a pole as a substitute toilet. What he should have done, however, was to be careful to check exactly what sort of pole it was that he had opted to wee against – because it turned out to be a live power pole.

Zzzzt, zzzzt!

Ouch!

The coroner's court in Darwin found that Sizzling Sammy had been accidentally electrocuted.

Pee is for power

A twenty-seven-year-old Thai man with a false leg found himself in the same situation as Sizzling Sammy years later in July 2003, when he felt the call of nature and selected a power pole alongside a main road in Bangkok.

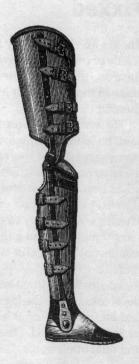

His father told police that they'd stopped their car near a tollbooth during a rainstorm. According to a story in the *Queensland Times* on 5 July 2003, the victim is thought to have peed on a flooded ground line, and the prosthesis, being made largely of metal, was a good conductor, and . . . well, you can guess the rest.

This Sporting Death

Sport takes its toll on the human frame – but sometimes it can be with deadly and unintended results.

Fixxed

There's an elegant irony in meeting your end at the hands of one of your own creations. It happened to Jim Fixx, the man reputed to have started the jogging craze in the 1970s with his *The Complete Book of Running*.

He was visiting Greensboro in Vermont when, it is said, he left the house and began his usual jog. After running for only a short distance he suffered a massive heart attack, which killed him. The post-mortem showed that one of his coronary arteries was severely clogged, a second more so, and a third was more clogged still at 99 per cent.

Fixx had had three attacks in the weeks before the jog that had brought on – or at least probably facilitated – the final and fatal one.

Not a barrel of laughs

When you've defied death several times for the sake of your (extreme) sport, dying of something as stupid as 'complications' can't be much fun.

Bobby Leech was a twentieth-century stuntman who took his sport seriously – so much so that he attempted a barrel ride over Niagara Falls in July 1911 and broke 'nearly every bone' in his body, according to contemporary reports.

Despite the seriousness of his injuries, he made a full recovery and, still in love with his daredevil lifestyle, set off on a worldwide lecture tour. All went well until he came to deliver a lecture in New Zealand, where he fell and broke a leg – just the one.

He later died of complications.

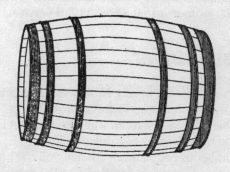

Frank's running jump

Extreme sports can lead to spectacular deaths, but in June 1999 things were a little more mundane for Frank Gambalie III when he took a running leap off the west wall of El Capitán cliff in California's Yosemite National Park. He knew that such parajumps were illegal, of course, but they happen all the time. Besides, beating the park rangers was all part of the fun.

When twenty-eight-year-old Gambalie took his flying jump, he was spotted by two rangers, and, after landing safely, he attempted to outrun them, but ended up drowning in the Merced River. He'd jumped into the river, which was still swollen from spring snowmelt, and tried to swim it. His body, which had been pinned beneath a rock about 300 feet from where he was last sighted, was recovered twenty-eight days later.

BASE jumping, as it's called (BASE standing for 'buildings, antennae, spans and earth' – the four main types of object from which the enthusiasts leap), is illegal in most national parks in the United States, but El Cap, as it's known, is something of a jewel in any BASE jumper's crown. Yosemite officials believe that about 100 jumpers use the park in this way each year.

Stupid surfer

It was the day of the Spring Nationals – a country festival – in Shepparton, Victoria, Australia, in November 2002, and a truck was being driven noisily along the high street at five miles an hour.

A number of people were climbing all over it, frolicking and generally entering into the spirit of the occasion. One man decided he'd engage in that favourite Aussie sport of surfing, but on dry land rather than on water.

Wearing a big Mexican hat, he tied a rope to the back of the truck and, with a can of beer in one hand, held on to the rope with the other and 'surfed' on a piece of cardboard along the surface of the road. Unfortunately, the rope became caught under the vehicle and he was somehow dragged beneath it, and became a human speed bump.

The picture on the front page of the newspaper the following day showed the body bag with the big Mexican hat beside it.

Gone fishin'

Harris Simwaba decided he'd like to do a spot of fishing one day in the early 1990s.

The twenty-eight-year-old Zambian made a decent catch in the Chungu River, about ten miles east of Livingstone, according to Zambian media, and had opted for the unusual method of trying to bite the fish to death, but it slid down his throat. When he tried to hook it with a stick, he could only manage to shove the thing further into his throat.

Villagers found him the following day on their way to their work in the fields. He was sprawled on the ground with a stick poking from his mouth, and as a villager took away the stick, the fish came out, too. It is unrecorded as to whether the locals took advantage of their unconventional fishy find, and cooked it for lunch.

All in a Day's Work

If it weren't for deaths at work, there'd be no need for the Health and Safety Executive. Some jobs are just dangerous, others shouldn't be, but they become so because they're done by . . . well, by humans. And humans can be very stupid.

Disappearing act

Magicians are famed for getting things just right, because that's how their tricks appear to work so seamlessly.

The famous American Lafayette (1872–1911), whose real name was Siegmund Neuberger, got things a little too right on one fateful occasion. He insisted that the 'pass door' – the small door leading from the stalls into the wings – should be kept locked during performances so that no one could get where they shouldn't and discover his secrets.

However, on 9 May 1911, when Lafayette was playing Edinburgh's Empire Theatre, a fire broke out in the building. He rushed to the pass door, but had forgotten that he'd asked for it to be locked. The stage was awash with flames before he could get to another exit, and he was overcome by fumes and died.

Death, where is thy sting?

The American physician Dr Jesse William Lazear (1866–1900) was a member of the Yellow Fever Commission in Cuba and was noted for his experiments associated with that crippling disease.

Lazear wanted to demonstrate that mosquitoes transmitted this horrendous disease, and in order to prove his theory, he allowed a mosquito to bite him. He contracted yellow fever, however, and died.

Concrete bungle

Two experienced construction workers in London were proud of their work. They had just drilled a hole through thick concrete in 1998, but hadn't realized they were standing inside the circle as the block of concrete gave way.

Both twenty-eight-year-old men fell 100 feet (30 metres) to their deaths eight storeys below. Neither had been wearing safety harnesses.

A fishy tale

When thirty-year-old Nakorn Hawthong was fishing in the Thai province of Uthai Thani, he caught a fish and put it between his teeth because he didn't have a basket to keep it in, and then he continued fishing. Unfortunately for Hawthong, the fish choked him to death.

The Thai man's death in November 1991 is not the only one of its kind. Thirty years before, according to a report in the *Canberra Times* of 11 February 1963, Mario Golfo, of Messina in Sicily, had tried to stun a small sole by biting its head, but was thwarted in his attempt when the scaly creature managed to wriggle into his throat and choke him.

Tall story

A lesson in how to give proper specifications when ordering manufactured goods is to be found in the story of Zimmerman, otherwise known as the Julich Giant.

Julich was the name of a Prussian town during the reign of King Frederick William I, a leader who liked his soldiers to be tall – preferably around 6 foot 6 inches (2 metres). So his agents would be dispatched to all corners of the land to seek out such immense specimens.

One day, in 1660, they happened upon Zimmerman, a carpenter, and asked him to make a wooden crate just a little taller than he was – which was almost 6 and a half feet. Zimmerman obliged, but the recruiting agent complained that it was too short. Nonsense, protested the lanky Zimmerman, so the agent told him to step inside to prove it. When Zimmerman obliged, the crate was quickly closed up and locked, and handed to a group of grenadiers to take back to HQ. Unfortunately, the agent who had told the carpenter how to construct the crate had omitted to mention the rather important issue of ventilation holes.

Consequently, this particular recruiting exercise was in vain: all they got for their efforts was Zimmerman's corpse.

A boy named Soo

As part of his act, stage magician Jung Ling Soo would 'catch' a marked bullet – but one evening he caught it for real.

The idea was that Jung – alias William Ellisworth Robinson – would appear to catch a marked bullet, satisfying the audience that it was the one 'fired' from a gun. However, on 23 March 1918 at the Empire Theatre in London's Wood Green, Jung wasn't prepared for the fact that a worn bit of the trick gun's mechanism had allowed some gunpowder to trickle into where it shouldn't have. A real bullet – presumably the one that a member of the audience would have been allowed to inspect beforehand – was thus fired, and Jung caught it. This time it was fatal.

Cunning stunts

Vic Rivers (1948–77) was a highly respected stuntman in the movie business. The stupid irony concerning his death is that he performed all kinds of seemingly death-defying escapades, and then met his end in the most anticlimactic of circumstances.

Rivers (sometimes credited as Victor Rivers) was a stuntman during the making of the biker movie *Hi-Riders* in 1977. One stunt – which turned out to be his last – had him driving his car off a bridge and performing a rollover in a three-foot stream bed. Unfortunately, the experience seemed to have dizzied him, because when he got out his car he keeled over, fell into the muddy water and drowned.

Rivers isn't the only stuntman to die in a comparatively mundane manner. On the set of *Steel* in 1978, A. J. Bakunas successfully executed a record high fall, but was killed when the seams on his airbag broke. Jack Coffer and Duck Bullock died in car crashes while on their way home from some dangerous stunt work, while another stuntman, Gene Coogan, died after falling asleep in bed with a lighted cigarette.

Hard to swallow

'The Human Ostrich' was the name given to Robert Naysmith, who died in an Islington workhouse in London in 1906.

Born in Montrose, Scotland, Naysmith alienated himself from his family and went on the road with a highly unusual show: swallowing things. Hatpins, stones, glass and nails were on his menu during the course of any evening, and, not surprisingly, his unusual appetites eventually took their toll.

He was thirty-four when he was forced to give up this unlikely profession, and he began made a small living selling bootlaces, but this did not earn him enough to avoid the workhouse. Eventually an abscess formed in his body, and when doctors lanced it a brass-headed nail was found. But it was too late to save him, and he died in the summer of 1906.

A post-mortem found an intriguing assortment of hatpins and nails in the kidneys, liver and intestines, and, although Naysmith's death was officially gastritis and peritonitis, the inquest jury, having heard of his exploits, recorded a verdict of death by misadventure.

Get out of *that*!

Getting punched in the guts was all in a day's work for the great American escapologist Harry Houdini (1874–1926). After all, he had the abdominal 'six-pack' to take it – well-defined, honed, hard muscles that could be contracted to withstand a punch from any fist.

This was all part of Houdini's stock-in-trade: he had begun his professional life as a trapeze artist and had then moved on to magic and escapology – and a well-developed body was just what was needed for that line of work.

But the student who hit Houdini was too stupid to realize that the great man needed to tense his muscles first – and he aimed a blow to the abdomen before the magician could prepare. Houdini subsequently suffered peritonitis and died.

Have gun, will kill myself

Clement Vallandigham became a lawyer after he had been banished to the American South after making speeches that attacked the administration of President Abraham Lincoln in 1863. He had been a well-known Northern Democrat, and had campaigned for states' rights during the American Civil War.

As a lawyer, his last appearance in a courtroom was a dramatic one. He was representing a man accused of murder, who was said to have shot a man. The fellow's defence was that the victim had drawn his own gun in such a way as to cause it to fire, thus killing himself.

Vallandigham thought a demonstration was in order, and pulled out the loaded evidence gun in court to show the jury how the gun would have been drawn. Unfortunately, it went off, and Vallandigham appeared in court no more.

It's not the only time people connected with the law have disposed of themselves during a re-enactment. Far more recently – in 1993, in Illinois – a similar thing happened to a police officer who was showing a colleague how a fellow cop had killed himself, and demonstrated the shooting a week after the tragedy.

But the officer – who had twenty years' experience as a police officer – forgot to unload the .357 Magnum before his demo, and shot himself in the stomach. The careless incident didn't cause his death, but as he drove himself to hospital he died in a car crash.

In vino very dead

Orfeo Agostinetto was a great amateur winemaker, and would make up to 500 gallons at a time. Although the Italian from Treviso didn't meet his maker through cirrhosis of the liver, it was the case that drinking to excess did play a part.

Orfeo had a few over the limit one evening and fell into the new vat that contained the new season's batch of wine – all 500 gallons of it. He ended up drowning in his potent produce.

Ghost rider

Charles Thornton, a carter, suffered a heart attack and died while driving a vanload of wood through London in 1916. At the time, though, no one knew, because he didn't fall off his seat, but remained upright with reins in hand.

So his team of horses trotted blithely on, while his pal Richard Dean continued to drive another van behind, unaware of his friend's demise. Only when they reached their destination – a timber yard – was Thornton's death discovered.

Leave well alone

It's an army rule: if you're doing exercises with bombs and there's a dud, leave it where it is. But one day in 1983 at the Fort Bragg Military Reservation in North Carolina, someone decided to flout the rule, and paid with his life.

It happened at the LAW (light, anti-tank weapon) range, where soldiers get to fire a real LAW round. Test rounds are smaller and not armed with the full explosive power of those used in warfare, but they're lethal nonetheless, with their orange chalk warhead making them look a little like a Guy Fawkes' Night sky rocket.

The range safety officer, Sergeant Lowe, along with three other men, had the job of setting up a moving target. They didn't have the right tools to install the target on the carrier, so they improvised, using a metal tent peg as a hammer.

While walking on the range, Lowe saw – and picked up – an M72A2 66mm LAW dud round that hadn't gone off when it hit the target. He was warned to leave it alone, but he dismissed it as 'just an old dud', and proceeded to hit it with the tent peg.

Bang!

The pressure-sensitive piezoelectric detonator was activated and the round exploded, killing Sergeant Lowe, who, as well as having his left arm and parts of his right hand blown off by the blast, also received fatal abdominal wounds.

Oven-ready

The microwave oven has been around for decades now, but some people still don't know how it works. Hence the stories that crop up from time to time of people who have put their pet pooch or moggy in one to dry off.

In the late 1990s, a Canadian nightwatchman from Thompson in Manitoba, was trying to keep warm next to a feed horn microwave (telecommunications dish) on Christmas Eve. Perhaps his employers should have known that something like this would happen, as he'd been suspended once before for breaking safety rules, according to a Northern Manitoba Signal Relay spokeswoman.

On this occasion, the nightwatchman told colleagues that the only way he could stay warm while working his twelve-hour shift – during which temperatures could dip to below 40°F (4.4°C) – was to stand in front of the dish. He took with him a twelve-pack of beer and a folding chair, and off he went to complete his shift, having not been told, apparently, that there would be a tenfold boost in power that day to cope with the expected hike in telecoms traffic.

Microwaves, as we all (should) know, are absorbed by moisture inside whatever is being cooked or heated. This misguided fellow must have thought they were radiant heatwaves, because the following day a colleague turned up to relieve him and smelled what he thought was a festive roast that the nightwatchman had prepared.

It wasn't.

Prim and improper

Spanish Prime Minister Juan Prim (1814–70) probably thought he'd got off lightly when a would-be assassin shot him as he rode down the Calle de Alcala in Madrid in 1870. After all, Prim received only a finger wound because of the gunman's suspect marksmanship.

However, what looked stupid to begin with turned out to be to the gunman's advantage, for the would-be assassin became an actual assassin after the Prime Minister's finger injury worsened, leading to amputation and then an infection of the stump, which in turn spread to other parts of the body, with the result that Prim was dead within a few days.

Safety first – not!

Surely if you're making a safety video, the first thing you'd think of would be safety?

In this case it would seem that Peter, the fifty-two-year-old owner of a machinery and equipment training school, wanted to get the film made all too quickly, and in doing so abandoned all common sense.

He was filming a forklift safety demonstration at the training school in Perth, Australia, in March 2000, when he was thrown from the cabin of his forklift, and crushed. Investigators later found that the fault had been entirely due to driver error: he'd been driving too quickly over varied terrain, and had not been wearing a seatbelt.

Look, no HANS

The HANS (head and neck safety) helmet-restraint system has been hailed by racing drivers, but not by Dale Earnhardt. He was dead against it.

According to the American racing journalist Ed Hinton, 'He once referred to the HANS device as, quote, "that damned noose". His common sense told him if you wore straps around your helmet and you got in a crash it was going to hang you. So he referred to it as the noose, because he thought it was going to kill him rather than save him . . .

'He sat right here in Indianapolis and he looked me in the eye and, with a lot of people present, he said, "I'm comfortable the way I've got my stuff rigged, and I have not pulled my brain stem loose and I've hit the wall many times. I have not pulled my brain stem loose" – his exact words . . . And I looked him back in the eye and my thought was, "Yet."'

Unfortunately, Dale Earnhardt hit a wall during the Daytona 500 in February 2001, sustaining a fatal fracture because, said the subsequent inquiry, he had a 'restrained torso but unrestrained head'.

NASCAR – America's National Association of Stock Car Auto Racing – made the device compulsory six months after Earnhardt's death.

Something fishy

In October 2002, a worker at the fish-sauce factory in Phan Thiet, a Vietnamese coastal town 118 miles (190 kilometres) north-east of Ho Chi Minh City, fell into the sauce tank. Unfortunately, when four other workers – including the unlucky man's wife – tried to rescue him, the fumes from the 7-foot- (2.2-metre-) deep tank overcame them. All five bodies lay in the bottom of tank before they could be dragged out. And still the killer sauce tank had not completed its grisly work, as one of the rescuers – a thirty-four-year-old man – also died later in hospital in Binh Thuan.

Just eight months later, a similar tragedy occurred when seven Egyptian workers drowned in a vat of animal blood at a slaughterhouse near the Red Sea port of Aqaba in Jordan. One man fell in, another tried to save him and the others all drowned, each trying to save the previous victim. The blood was too thick and clotted to swim in, according to an Associated Press report of 13 August 2003.

Swede and peas

In 2002 rescue workers were unable to revive a thirty-year-old Swede who had just been buried under a 13-tonne pile of peas.

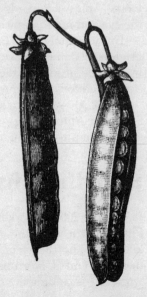

It happened in a storage silo in Mjölby, south-eastern Sweden, and he was working on an electrical installation there when the peas were accidentally dumped on him.

Tanked up

Brazilian Manoel Messias Batista Coelho used to clean out the storage tanks of tanker lorries that carried petrol – until January 2003, when he momentarily forgot what the tanks contained.

The thirty-five-year-old worker would fill a tanker with water as a safety procedure to force the flammable vapour out of the tank. One day, he began this practice, nipped off and returned an hour later to see if the water had risen to the top. But it was so dark in there that he needed a light to help him see more clearly. He decided to use his cigarette lighter to access the situation, but the problem was that the water hadn't reached a high enough level to have expelled all the fumes, and so the inevitable happened.

What's in a name?

If you had been named Please Shoot Me you might not wish to cross any border posts. But certain names can cause problems for their owners, as the French general Count Valavoir found to his cost.

This seventeenth-century noble soldier – who served under the French marshal who distinguished himself during the Thirty Years' War, Henri de La Tour d'Auvergne Turenne, no less – was challenged in a camp on a dark night by a sentinel from his own side. All he could answer in response to the demand for his name was 'Valavoir', which sounds rather similar to 'va le voir' (or 'go and see').

The sentinel duly took offence and shot the count dead, thinking he was an enemy.

Through a glass fatally

A lawyer plunged twenty-four floors to his death in Toronto in July 1993 after demonstrating the strength – or lack of it – of a safety window.

The thirty-nine-year-old fell into the courtyard of the Toronto Dominion Bank Tower, according to a police spokesman, after he had been discussing the toughness of the building's windows to a group of visiting law students. Police said he'd previously conducted similar demonstrations – but this one proved fatal after he went through the glass.

She got the point

Did you hear the one about the little lad who went to the variety theatre with his parents, and, on seeing the antics of the knife thrower and his attractive assistant, said to his mother, 'It's a swizz: he hasn't hit her once yet'?

He wouldn't have been disappointed on the occasion when Julia Bernard was the assistant to a knife thrower in a vaudeville stage show in New York in the late nineteenth century. What Julia – who was also a singer and dancer – did not know that on this night in 1890 she would be performing her last.

Thud! One knife landed just shy of her left arm.

Thud! Another just missed her right arm.

Thud, thud! The same for each leg.

Then came time for the knife thrower to miss her head. But he didn't.

The knife pierced Julia Bernard's forehead and entered her brain. She died instantly.

Friends and Family

We were going to call this one 'Family Feuds', then 'Happy Families', but realized that friends, too, can be unfriendly at times – even though it's often by accident.

The balcony scene

It was hardly comparable to the dramatic moment played out by Shakespeare's star-crossed lovers, but the incident that occurred in the working-class neighbourhood of Boedo in Buenos Aires, in 1998, during a fierce marital dispute, did concern a young man and his love – and a balcony.

At one point during the argument, the twenty-five-year-old man picked up his twenty-year-old wife and flung her off the balcony, which was eight floors up, but she didn't die: instead she got tangled up in some power lines. Whether he was hit by feelings of remorse or simply wanted to finish the job, he inexplicably dived after her. Unfortunately, he missed the power lines and fell to his death.

His wife – or rather, widow – had managed to swing to the safety of a nearby balcony.

Bridge too far

John G. Bennett's death seemed to be on the cards. He and his wife Myrtle, of Kansas City, were great bridge enthusiasts, but such was their dedication to their skill in playing the game that they were prone to argue at the table.

They were playing with another couple one evening at the Bennetts' home, and the visitors were curling their toes in embarrassment as Myrtle and John slugged it out – verbally at this point – over some perceived blunder John had committed concerning a trump or a trick. But the argument grew more fierce, with Myrtle accusing John of being a 'bum bridge player'. So he slapped her face.

Off she dashed into the bedroom: not for a good cry, though, but to get a revolver, with which she promptly shot John across the table.

She was acquitted of first-degree murder at her trial in 1929. The American writer and broadcaster Alexander Woolcott, claimed that, some years later, Myrtle was at the bridge table again, when her partner committed an error. Jokingly, he turned to Myrtle and said, 'You'll shoot me for this.' According to Woolcott, Myrtle just fainted.

Magnum opus

They don't come much more bizarre than the circumstances surrounding the death of one Ronald Opus in March 1994.

According to a story told by Dr Don Harper Mills, president of the American Association for Forensic Science, at its 1994 awards dinner, Opus jumped from a tenth-storey window, intending to commit suicide. Mills told the audience that a safety net had been installed just below the eighth floor to protect building workers. So Opus would not have succeeded in his suicide after all.

However, as he passed the ninth floor, an elderly man and woman were arguing in an apartment, and the man was threatening his wife with a shotgun, which was discharged. The bullets missed the woman completely, but passed through the open window and killed Ronald Opus.

Mills said that, ordinarily, the death was still suicide, because Opus had intended to kill himself, although the medical examiner plumped for homicide, because when someone intends to kill one person but kills a someone in the attempt, he or she is guilty of murdering the second party.

The twist in the tale that gives this story its bizarre quality is that the elderly gent said it was his longstanding habit to threaten his wife with an unloaded shotgun, and so he had no intention of killing her. Therefore, the killing of Opus was an accident, because the gun had been accidentally loaded.

It doesn't end there, either, because it turned out that the couple's son had loaded the shotgun a few weeks before this incident, because his mother had cut off his finances. Being aware of his father's habit of threatening his wife with the gun, the son had loaded it, thinking the old man would shoot the old woman. So it was no longer an accident, and the murder of Ronald Opus was back on the agenda.

The weirdest thing of all, though, was that investigators discovered that the old couple's son turned out to be one Ronald Opus. It transpired that he had become so depressed over his failure to bring about his mother's death that he jumped off the building – only to be killed by shotgun pellets (that he himself had placed in his father's gun) on the way down.

Eventually, the medical examiner settled on a verdict of suicide.

Fatal landing

Vera Czermak, a Czechoslovakian, learned that her husband was seeing another woman, and this made her suicidal. So she decided to do the deed by throwing herself out of her third-floor window in November 1992.

The story doesn't end there, however, for Vera's decision to end her own life also gave her unexpected revenge on the unfaithful Mr Czermak, who happened to be walking beneath the window at the time . . .

Vera was merely injured and recovered in hospital, but her husband's philandering ways came to a stop then and there when he unknowingly broke his wife's fall and met an untimely end in the process.

Fiery temper

According to *The Book of Lists*, the English nobleman and writer Eric Magnus Andreas Harry Stenbock (1860–95) decided that a poker was the most suitable – and probably the handiest – weapon when, for some reason, he needed to attack a friend.

When he grabbed it, however, he promptly fell into the fireplace and subsequently died of his burns.

A Tsar is . . . er dead

It can, on occasions, be downright stupid not to do as you are told, even if what you are told to do is to abdicate as the Tsar of Russia.

Tsar Paul I (1754–1801) met his end by such a show of stubbornness early in the nineteenth century. He was a capricious sort, although some of his acts had been rather progressive: political prisoners were freed and conscription was abolished, and the work owed by serfs to their owners was ended. Perhaps it was acts such as these that led to a his unpopularity among court nobility.

As he was retiring to bed on 23 March, three of his ministers – Benningsen, Zouboff and Pahlen – called on him in his own bedroom, and asked him if he would mind abdicating, or rather they suggested to him that it would be in best his interests to do so. In what turned out to be an ill-advised decision, he refused.

The family feud behind this story concerns the fact that his successor and son, Alexander I, is thought to have supported the plot to unseat his father, on condition that Paul's life would be spared. It wasn't: the three ministers strangled him.

Thanks for the gun, son

Most people remember Marvin Gaye for his soul music, both sung and written, and they may also have a vague recollection that he was shot by his dad. But there was a twist to the tale.

Gaye, who was born Marvin Pentz Gay, Jr in 1939 in Washington, DC, was struggling with drug addiction later in life, and moved back into his parents' home in Los Angeles.

On 1 April 1984, he attacked his father for verbally abusing his mother. His father was a preacher who had often beaten his children for minor 'offences', and his response to Marvin's intervention was to pick up a gun and shoot him. He was eventually convicted of voluntary manslaughter and given five years' probation. After his arrest, doctors examined him and found a cancerous tumour at the base of his brain, which it was conjectured may have had a bearing on his behaviour. When Gay, Sr was asked whether he loved his son Marvin, he said, 'Let's say that I didn't dislike him.'

Now here is the irony: the disciplinarian preacher would never have had a gun in the first place had Marvin not bought it as a gift some months before.

Death by braggadocio

It's well known that you can't kill a man from Invercargill, the southernmost city in the world. At least, that's what Roy Barton said, but he ended up being knifed for his boasting.

There was more to it than that, however, as Barton – who hailed from the New Zealand South Island city – blithely ignored the fact that Tina, the love of his life, came from a violent family; her mother having been tried and convicted of knifing to death her own husband thirty-three years previously.

Like Tina's own parents' marriage, her union with Roy was not a happy one. On April Fools' Day 1977 they had the mother of all rows, with Roy calling Tina a 'childless bitch' because she couldn't conceive, and adding, just for good measure, that she was the 'daughter of a whore and a murderess'. He then dared her to kill him, remarking how this would be impossible because 'you can't kill an Invercargill man'.

But she did it – by stabbing him thirty-six times through the heart. She was put on trial in Christchurch, New Zealand, in the same court in which her mother had been tried. In the end Tina was convicted not of murder but of manslaughter, after the jury had concluded that she'd been provoked by her macho husband's braggadocio.

Premature burial

Langley Collier (1886–1947) was an eccentric American collector of all kinds of things, and was also something of a recluse.

One day, while taking food to his brother Homer – who was also a solitary character – Langley tripped the burglar trap. Instantly, he was buried under several breadboxes, bundles of newspapers, a suitcase filled with metal and a sewing machine, which crushed him to death.

So reliant was the reclusive Homer on his brother's help that without Langley's vital food deliveries he starved to death. The bodies remained in the house for three weeks before they were found.

Musical Deaths

Well, it beats Musical Chairs for interest.
These deaths concern either musicians or
composers. Homer Simpson might say,
'That brings us back to doh!' Perhaps not.

Not singing, but drowning

The opera singer Brian
Sullivan (1918–69) was
understandably
disappointed when he
was asked to take the
role of understudy in
Wagner's
Götterdämmerung in
Switzerland. After all,
he'd sung the
eponymous part in
Britten's *Peter Grimes*,
which was quite an
accolade.

It's said that when he
didn't find an
opportunity to sing in
this production of
Wagner's huge music
drama – the fourth in the
Ring cycle – he drowned
himself, just as Peter
Grimes had done.

Unready Eddie

Twenty-one is no age to die, but that's the age at which one of the greatest jazz guitarists of his era shuffled off this mortal coil.

However, it wasn't the bout of tonsilitis that killed Eddie Lang (musical partner of the violinist Joe Venuti) in 1933, but a botched operation. Lang (born Salvatore Massaro in 1902) was a pal of Bing Crosby, who was very upset by Lang's death – not only because he had lost a good friend, but because it was Crosby who had urged Lang to have the operation in the first place . . .

Dogged by bad luck

The American composer Wallingford Riegger (1885–1961) was noted for well-crafted and very expressive music in contrapuntal atonal style; the sort of sound, in fact, that probably goes through your head when you hit a kerbstone.

Whether it did or not on the day of his own demise, we'll never know, but one day in 1961 Riegger was walking his dog along Columbus Avenue, New York, his pooch took a dislike to another four-legged stroller, and there was a canine punch-up. During the altercation, the dogs' leads became wrapped around Riegger's legs, and he tripped, dying from head injuries.

Heavy reading

Surely a man who was nimble-footed enough to write music for the pedal piano would be able to get out of the way of a toppling bookcase? Unfortunately for Charles-Valentin Alkan (1813–88), he didn't quite manage it.

Alkan (real name Morhange) was a friend of Liszt and Chopin, among others, and wrote virtuoso piano music that predated the work of Liszt and Brahms. Much of the footwork involved in his works is intricate, to say the least – often as complex as the fingering. Indeed, some of his output was in the form of four-part fugues for pedals alone. As well as producing some of the most technically forbidding music around, Alkan was a misanthropic, eccentric recluse who had become known as a virtuoso by the age of seventeen.

But one day, when reaching for a copy of the Talmud from a high shelf, the bookcase fell on him with an unmusical clatter and killed him.

Parting shot

The soprano Gertrude Bindernagel (1894–1932) was
shot by her second husband – for erroneous reasons,
as it turned out.

After a performance of Wagner's *Siegfried in Berlin*,
she was walking through the opera arcade when
Wilhelm Hintze, a banker, fired a gun at her at point-
blank range. She died some days later.

At the trial it emerged that Hintze was having
money worries, caused by economic uncertainties just
before the Nazis took power. He believed that his wife
and her lover were responsible for organizing a
conspiracy against him, but there was no conspiracy,
and there was no lover.

Spot of bother

The Russian composer and pianist Aleksandr
Nikolayevich Scriabin (1872–1915) created an
atmosphere of mystical yearning with his music,
which had great rhythmic complexity. But his death
was not to match the glory of his life's work.

This composer of such works as *The Divine Poem*
(1903) and *The Poem of Ecstasy* (1908) died from
scratching a pimple on his lip. This simple act led to
blood poisoning. What a stupid way to go.

Death by Death

Essentially a section on miscellaneous
deaths, this collection of untimely demises
is something of a pot pourri.

Prickly situation

There are some cacti that it's better to avoid having an
argument with – assuming you're into arguing with
cacti, that is. In 1982, just north of Lake Pleasant,
David Grundman, from Phoenix, Arizona, fired both
barrels of his twelve-bore at a giant saguaro, but it cost
him his life.

Saguaros are humungous plants, growing as high
as 50 feet (15 metres). They're also quite hardy brutes,
too, living as long as 150 or even 200 years.
Grundman's shotgun blast caused a 23-foot (7-metre)
section of the huge succulent to fall on him, crushing
him to death. The giant was about 26 feet (8 metres)
high and estimated to be about 100 years old. He had
already shot a smaller saguaro so many times
that it thudded to the ground. 'The first one
was easy,' he is reported to have said to his
pal, James Joseph Suchochi.

There's a song by the Texas rock band
the Austin Lounge Lizards that
chronicles Grundman's death.

Ants decked

First it was fruit that came hurtling out of the sky –
then something a bit heavier: furniture. In 1996, three
unfortunate people were killed by flying furniture as
they walked on the pavement near a hotel.

Two kids – a seven-year-old boy and his six-year-
old sister – had been left alone in their twenty-
seventh-floor hotel room while their parents had gone
off to the hotel's gaming room. The children, naturally,
were bored rigid. So they looked out of the window
and were fascinated by the 'ant-looking things' way
down below. They decided to squish them.

They started by throwing fruit, but, hey, that's
boring. So that's when they graduated to chairs and
tables, a television set and drawers from the dresser in
the bedroom, and ended up killing the three
unfortunate 'ants' on the ground below, who were
definitely in the wrong place at the wrong time.

Eau, dear!

The English novelist, playwright, drama critic and
essayist Arnold Bennett (1867–1931) wanted to prove a
point. But he paid for it with his life.

The author of such works
as *Anna of the Five Towns* (1902)
and *The Old Wives' Tale* (1908),
set out to show by example
that the drinking water in
Paris was all right to drink.
Unfortunately it turned out
not to be all right, and he died
of typhoid.

Going down!

When Raymond R. Foard arrived home at his apartment building in Maryland in 1977, he dug deep in his pockets, cursing the fact that he'd left his keys somewhere. Rather than waste time calling for help, he decided to scale the building all the way to the seventh floor in order to climb in through his apartment window.

He made it to the fifth, puffing and panting, when he was heard by a woman who was sitting on her balcony. Not surprisingly, she was terrified when she saw a hand grasp the edge of the balcony, and she did what many people would do in these circumstances: she screamed.

Unfortunately, the petrified yell broke Foard's concentration, and he lost his grip, plummeting down to the concrete – and his death – below.

He got the massage

Auckland's massage parlour was a favourite fortnightly haunt of a retired chef called George Wallace. The seventy-two-year-old New Zealander enjoyed the attentions of a number of pretty masseuses, who called him Old Wally, but eventually he chose a favourite masseuse – who was just seventeen, an amateur, who was paying for her college course using the money she earned from the parlour.

On a February afternoon in 1977, at the climax of his session, things proved too much for George, and he just sat up, screamed, and then fell back on to the table – dead.

Windy city

When your life's under threat; when you really ought to get away from a place because things are becoming dangerous; when it would be clearly rather silly to remain while Nature is in the process of hurling one of her deadliest weapons at you – well, why not stay and party!

Hurricane Camille claimed 143 lives along the Mississippi Gulf Coast in August 1969, but twenty of her victims had been attending a beachfront 'Hurricane Party' at the time of her gusty arrival.

There had been warnings aplenty telling people to evacuate the area, but these partygoers decided their festivities should continue unabated. They said that the concrete foundation of their apartment block and the second-floor location of their party gave them enough protection from the coming hurricane, but that was before a 24-foot wave smashed into the apartment. The entire building was destroyed. Partygoers then found themselves facing gale-force winds and brutal ocean surges.

Most died, but a few were swept miles away and, miraculously, survived.

Death in slow motion

A giant wave of treacle was responsible for twenty-one deaths and 150 injuries in Boston, Massachusetts, in January 1919. It might be said that the hapless victims came to a sticky end . . .

There was a tank filled to capacity with the stuff – 2,320,000 gallons or about 14,000 tons. The weather was unseasonably warm that January and caused the tank to burst. A thirty-foot wall of goo smashed buildings and threw horses, wagons and pool tables about as if they were playthings. Rescue efforts were hampered by the sheer stickiness of the molasses, because anyone trying to help just got caught up in it.

The next day, this appeared in the *New York Times:*

> A dull, muffled roar gave but an instant's warning before the top of the tank was blown into the air. The circular wall broke into two great segments of sheet iron which were pulled in opposite directions. Two million gallons of molasses rushed over the streets and converted into a sticky mass the wreckage of several small buildings which had been smashed by the force of the explosion.
>
> The greatest mortality apparently occurred in one of the city buildings where a score of municipal employees were eating their lunch. The building was demolished and the wreckage was hurled 50 yards [45 metres]. The other city building, which had an office on the ground floor and a tenement above, was similarly torn from its foundations.
>
> One of the sections of the tank wall fell on the firehouse which was nearby. The building was crushed and three firemen were buried in the ruins.

There are people in Boston who maintain they can still smell the stuff on a hot summer's day.

First, the good news . . .

When you're stuck in a psychiatric hospital at the beginning of the twentieth century, you could do with a bit of cheering up. Imagine how cheerful the Italian poet Severiano Ferrari must have felt when someone popped into his room in 1905, and said, 'Hey, Sevy, you've just been made professor of literature at the University of Bologna!'

Tragically, the news came as a bit of a shock to Ferrari. He had a heart attack and died.

Smoking can damage your health

The avant-garde composer Anton Von Webern (1883–1945) – who extended the twelve-tone system of the Austrian composer Arnold Schoenberg – was around in the days before health warnings appeared on cigarette packets. Not that it would have applied to his particular mode of demise – although it was a wish for a leisurely drag on the weed that caused it.

In September 1945, Webern stepped outside his home in Austria to smoke a cigarette, taking a stroll as he did so. Soon he found himself face to face with a military police officer belonging to the American occupying forces.

The MP shouted, 'Stop!' But for some reason, Webern – probably with his mind on rhythms and tone colours for his next intended dissonant piece of music – thought the officer had told him to advance. This crucial lack of comprehension on his part led to his being shot and killed on the spot.

Home and away

So security-conscious was a man from Grahamstown in South Africa that he asked police to guard his house while he was away. He would be back home, he said, on 12 January 1992.

However, on 30 December, almost a fortnight before the householder was due back, police noticed lights in the house, according to a report from the Associated Press that month. A police officer went round the back and stealthily approached the door, when it suddenly flew open. The officer opened fire, killing the 'intruder' instantly.

But it was no intruder: the householder had returned early.

In at the shallow end

A guy in Houston, Texas, was very proud of his new swimming pool, which he'd had installed in his back garden in June 1998.

A few weeks later, he and some friends were celebrating the Fourth of July, and the alcohol was flowing. At one point the pool's owner decided he'd climb onto the patio roof in order to dive into the water.

He was 6 foot (1.8 metres) tall while the water was only 4 foot (1.2 metres) deep. Consequently he broke his neck and died the following December.

During the interim, he and his family had tried to sue the installers on the grounds of faulty installation and inappropriate location – even though the pool owner had chosen the site himself.

Minding his pees and qs

The great Danish astronomer Tycho Brahe (1546–1601) may have paved the way for the equally great Sir Isaac Newton (1642–1727) to formulate a theory of gravity, but he didn't have the sense to break with tradition when he was bursting for a pee.

Brahe was a talented astronomer, and, although his theory was flawed, it nevertheless paved the way for planetary motion to be correctly described by the likes of Johannes Kepler (1571–1630), who was Brahe's pupil. For all his brilliance, though, poor old Tycho forgot to attend to a small but very important matter before going to his last banquet. He didn't have a pee.

It was considered impolite – an insult, even – to leave the table at a banquet before the meal was finished. As Tycho enjoyed a tipple, it was to prove greatly damaging to the unfortunate bladder condition with which he suffered.

Because he'd failed to 'go' before the meal, and was too polite to ask to be permitted to use the facilities once the proceedings had begun, he was forced to suffer in silence, crossing and uncrossing his legs under the table and no doubt speaking through gritted teeth. Unfortunately, his bladder could stand it no longer, and it burst, leaving him to die painfully over the next eleven days.

The dread flag

Boonchai Lotharakphong thought his flag would ward off bad luck, and so when the forty-three-year-old Thai factory owner hit money problems in November 2003, what better way to resolve them?

So up onto the roof of his factory went Mr Lotharakphong – but as he tried to raise his 'lucky' flag he slipped off the roof in Lopburi province, and fell to his death.

Cold comfort

Look after the pennies, they say, and the pounds will look after themselves. Well, it didn't quite work out that way for the billionaire founder of Canada's Weston food empire, George Weston.

Legend has it that he caught pneumonia because he had walked through a blizzard rather than pay for overnight accommodation or a taxi ride home in 1924.

The sound of silence

General William Henry Harrison (1773–1841), who became the ninth president of the USA in 1841, was a strange fellow indeed. He had the nickname 'General Mum', because he rode into battle – and subsequent glory – without saying a word during the War of 1812 between America and Britain.

However, during his inauguration as President in March 1841, he was not so taciturn: he made the longest inaugural speech in American history, which lasted nearly two hours, and was about 8,450 words in length.

Rather stupidly, though, it was delivered during a snowfall, and Harrison was wearing neither hat nor coat. It is said that the pneumonia that eventually killed him only a month after his inauguration was the result of this needlessly foolish action.

Even during the hours leading up to his death, he said nothing, according to *The Times* of 29 April 1841. 'In the course of the evening he became speechless,' the newspaper reported. 'About this time he was asked by Dr Hill if he was aware of his situation; he signified that he was. He then continued to sink very fast up to the time he expired.'

The luck of the Irish

Things were a bit too violent in her native Belfast for seventy-eight-year-old Elizabeth McClelland. With too many street fights it was getting a little too dangerous, so off she went to find a new life in Christchurch, on New Zealand's South Island.

A couple of years passed, when one day McClelland was taken to hospital where she died of head injuries after having been struck by a placard that someone had been carrying on a demonstration – in favour of Irish civil rights.

Pack of jokers

Poor William Pitcairn was just the sort of chap who'd welcome a drink. He was a tramp in nineteenth-century Staffordshire and was killed by a bunch of jokers, although probably not deliberately.

They plied him with several pints of ale and, not surprisingly, Pitcairn became somewhat inebriated. As a result he didn't really mind – in his stupefied state – being put into the local stocks for a laugh. His feet were fixed firmly to the apparatus, and he couldn't move – and that was where he was found the next morning – dead from exposure and malnutrition.

The poacher poached

A poacher got a taste of his own medicine after he had been electrocuting fish in a lake in central Poland in 1995. The twenty-four-year-old man was in a party of four who were fishing with a cable that linked a net and a high-voltage electricity line.

The PAP news agency reported an official of Włocławek as saying, 'For a while everything went according to the poachers' plan and they had fish in their bags. But at a certain moment the man holding the net tripped and fell into the water.'

And there he was poached – or at least electrocuted. The other poachers tried to revive him, but it was too late.

Dead unlucky

Lady Luck was just not on Edward Danvers's side as he passed the Brooks coffee shop in London. In the eighteenth century this popular coffee house was the haunt of countless men of fashion, many of whom were young bloods, who were noted for their willingness to gamble on just about anything. On this occasion it was poor Edward Danvers who gave them the opportunity they were looking for by presenting them with an unusual subject for a bet.

As he walked past the establishment Danvers suddenly collapsed on the street, and the smart young men in the coffee shop immediately opened a book on whether he would live or die. No one could help him, of course, because they reasoned that this would interfere with the odds. Those who bet that he would die were lucky; Edward Danvers was not.

Wish you were here

This is the tale of a stupid death that wasn't a death, but the tale's worth telling, because, had the dear lady concerned been of a weaker disposition, she might well have dropped dead of shock.

She was the wife of a rector who had just died, and she received an email from a US businessman who had the same first name as her deceased husband. The fellow had travelled south to sunny Florida for work reasons, and his wife was due to follow the next day.

When he got to his hotel room the businessman emailed his wife. Because he had left his address book on his desktop computer at home, he typed in what he thought was her email address, but he had got one letter wrong, and so the message went off to someone of a similar name: the rector's widow. When she read the message, she is said to have fainted when she saw it, thinking it was from her late hubby.

This is roughly what the email said:

Dearest Wife

Have just checked in. Preparations all made for your arrival tomorrow.

Love John

PS. It sure is hot down here . . .

You must be choking!

An anonymous Polish immigrant in Stoke-on-Trent managed to prove something that Professor Van Helsing had said years before: garlic keeps vampires away. The Pole managed to prove it – but in 1973 it cost him his life.

The man had an irrational fear of vampires, and so slept each night with a clove of garlic in his mouth. He did this for years – and, sure enough, the vampires stayed away. However, one night he began coughing in his sleep, and in doing so he dislodged the clove of garlic, which caught in his throat and choked him to death.

Truly amazing!

Amazing Joe Burrus, an American escape artist and magician, was also a recovering drug addict who wanted to give something back to society.

So, in 1990, he decided to perform a stunt worthy of the great Harry Houdini for the benefit of a rehabilitation clinic. He was to be bound in chains and placed in a locked coffin before being covered by a mound of dirt and wet cement to a depth of about two metres.

In the event about nine tonnes of this gloop was poured onto the coffin, but it wasn't his escapology skills that let him down. It was simply that the coffin couldn't stand up to the weight of the load – with the result that Amazing Joe Burrus was crushed to death.

Holy Eiffel Tower, Batman!

A French tailor called Teichelt was several decades ahead of Batman creator Bob Kane. He devised a bat-wing cape that he thought would enable him to fly, and he asked the Paris authorities to allow him to leap from the Eiffel Tower.

The authorities weren't too keen, but they gave permission eventually, with the proviso that Teichelt would also request police authorization and sign a document absolving tower authorities from any blame should anything go wrong. Which it did. Spectacularly.

The police duly gave their permission and so Teichelt, accompanied by some well-wishers and journalists, climbed to the level of the first platform.

He stepped off the edge . . . and plunged to his death.

You're choking, of course!

An unidentified man was probably a little the worse for drink as he watched the sinuous movements of an exotic dancer at a club in Phillipsburg, New Jersey, one night in 1998.

Eventually, he just couldn't help himself, and after plucking a pasty from her, which she had been using as part of her act, he bit into it. But the trouble was, it wasn't meant to be eaten. In fact it was covered in sequins, and he choked to death.

The dancer, identified only as Ginger, said, 'I didn't think he was going to eat it. He was really drunk.'

One-way shootout

In March 2003, three robbers decided to invade the bar in a Madrid brothel one morning, but they were still there when police got a call that an incident was in progress. When the officers surrounded the building and began to use a megaphone to encourage the occupants to come out, so afraid were they of being arrested that the intruders decided that the best way out was to shoot . . . and to shoot some more . . . at everything and everyone in sight. They would either escape or die in a blaze of glory.

Naturally, the police fired back, killing two of the robbers and wounding a third in his right leg. Baffled, the police wondered why they'd managed to win the day so easily – and then discovered that the raiders had been using real guns which were loaded with blank ammunition. Presumably the criminals had hoped to use the guns to create fear and thus carry out their intended robbery without actually killing anyone.

Inner cleansing

When Herbert Pickney, a born-again Christian, decided to end it all in a Charleston jail in South Carolina in July 1992, he must have decided that he was unclean in the eyes of the Lord. His chosen method of dispatch was the consumption of eight bars of soap and five cans of shaving cream. He died several hours later.

According to the *Weekly News* of 25 July, before he died he informed his warders: 'The Lord told me to do it.'

Heart of the matter

Some tribal peoples have been known to believe that, if you eat part of a person, you will acquire attributes which reflect that particular body part. Perhaps this was what one Dr Buckland had in mind when he took an interest in the preserved heart of King Louis XIV of France.

It was once possible to view the heart of Louis XIV – who was known as the Sun King, and who died in 1715. It had been donated to the Harcourt family as thanks from a French cleric for the family's provision of hospitality to refugee French nobles during the Revolution. Generations of the Harcourts passed on this relic – which looked like a piece of dried-up leather – and in 1905, when Dr Buckland, Dean of Westminster, was visiting, he was shown the royal heart.

He was fascinated by it, and wet his finger and rubbed it on the organ, thence licking the digit clean. Then he picked up the heart, shoved it into his mouth and swallowed it whole (although it's uncertain as to whether this was deliberate or accidental).

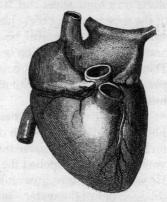

Whatever had motivated Buckland to do such a thing, the cleric died some time later – and the heart, far from being life-giving, was death-inducing.

Poleaxed

Woodrow W. Creekmore of Chickasha, Oklahoma, was a lucky man – for a while.

After a tie rod had broken on his car while he was driving near his home town in 1976, the vehicle careered into a telegraph pole. Woody was lucky: he walked away alive.

However, some time later he was having a friendly chat with the Highway Patrol officer who had come to investigate the accident, when the pole fell over, landing right on Creekmore's head and killing him.

Got there in the end

What makes this death so stupid is that the very unstupid Jacques LeFevrier planned his own demise in 1999 with military precision, but still managed not to kill himself in the way he'd intended.

The Frenchman tied a noose around his neck and stood on a high, sheer cliff, having tied the other end of the rope to a large rock. Just in case this method of suicide wasn't successful, he also drank some poison, and as an extra precaution he set fire to his clothes. Then, as an extra, extra precaution, he produced a pistol to shoot himself with as he jumped. But he missed.

The bullet cut through his rope instead, and he plunged into the sea, which duly put out the flames on his burning clothes. He then suffered a fit of vomiting, which expelled the poison he'd swallowed. He was saved from drowning when a fisherman dragged out of the water – but, his efforts not wholly in vain, he later died of hypothermia.

Road Kill

Our roads don't become safer. The world over, they become ever more congested, and that usually means prangs and road rage and just plain bizarre happenings that sometimes result in stupid deaths.

Dying to be famous

Some people will kill to get into the book of *Guinness World Records*, and some will sacrifice their own lives in the attempt.

Baldwin Street in Dunedin, New Zealand, was listed as the steepest street in the world, and two university students decided that a pell-mell ride down this 38-degree incline would be just the thing to make it into the record books. So, in the early hours of the morning one day in early 2000, Ana and her friend got hold of a two-wheeled rubbish bin and climbed in, pushing themselves off and into a wheeling-slide down the hill, before crashing into a legally parked trailer almost 55 yards (50 metres) from their starting point.

Ana was killed instantly, and her friend suffered serious head injuries.

Furthermore, the reckless run didn't make the record books because there was no way of knowing what sort of speed they had reached.

A time to die

A group of Palestinian terrorists became the unwitting victims of the change from daylight-saving time in 1999, after Israel had imposed a premature switch from DST to standard time, to accommodate a week of pre-sunrise prayers.

The Palestinians had decided not to validate 'Zionist Time' by using it, and therefore no one knew the 'correct' time in Palestine for about a week.

So at 5.30 p.m. on Sunday, when two car bombs exploded, the terrorists transporting the bombs were killed. They had been coordinated to go off at this time in different cities, but the bombs had been primed in a Palestine-controlled area and set to go off in DST. The drivers, however, had already switched to standard time and, when they loaded the bombs on board their cars, they didn't synchronize their watches to the correct standard of time.

Off her head

On 29 June 1967, sexy actress Jayne Mansfield was killed when a car driven by her lover Sam Brody crashed into a parked truck, causing the roof of the car to be sheared off completely. Both were killed instantly.

Contrary to rumours started by the press, Mansfield was not decapitated in the accident. The large blonde bouffant wig she had been wearing certainly flew off during the collision, but her head remained firmly attached to her body, a fact that was later verified by her undertaker.

Hello, I'm on a train line

It's a crime for drivers to use mobile phones while driving their car, and so perhaps the same should apply to people on foot as well.

In August 2002, Kansas police reported that a man from Olathe had been killed by a train after his own vehicle had broken down. Presumably it had come to a standstill on a level crossing, but no – it was simply stuck on Interstate 35. What he had done – it was said by police – was to walk away from his car and venture on to a railway track with his mobile phone clamped to his ear as he called for help.

The train driver said the man had been holding the phone to one ear and cupping the other with his hand to block out the surrounding noise. Unfortunately, the main cause of the surrounding noise was the sound of the oncoming train – which, of course, was unable to stop in time.

Give us a brake!

In 1989 E. Frenkel was a Soviet illusionist and mentalist back before he met his end.

Convinced that he could stop vehicles with the power of his mind alone, he began to demonstrate his skill starting with bicycles and small cars, though just what success he had – and how much it was down to the drivers' feelings of sympathy for him – will never be known.

However, one day in September that year, Frenkel decided on the ultimate test: he would stop a train in – or, rather, on – its tracks. But the problem was that he didn't succeed. The engine driver couldn't apply the brakes in time when he saw Frenkel on the tracks, having thrown his briefcase aside, standing with arms raised, head down and an intense expression of concentration on his face.

Not surprisingly, the inevitable happened, with the result that Frenkel had flexed his mental muscles for the last time.

Plane stupid

Maybe this doesn't qualify as road kill as such, but we can stretch a point, because it happened on a runway to someone using road transport.

It happened in December 1997 when a twenty-five-year-old cyclist called Marcelo was crossing a runway in Sorocaba, 54 miles (87 kilometres) away from São Paulo, Brazil. He wasn't able to hear the oncoming landing aeroplane because he was wearing headphones plugged into his Walkman. The fatal end result was inevitable.

Look before you leap

Understandably programmed for self-preservation, Marco decided that his first duty was to jump out of his Dodge van when he realized that his brakes had failed while driving down an Idaho mountain road with eight passengers in July 2001.

So he leaped from the vehicle.

However, things didn't turn out as badly as Marco anticipated – well, not for the passengers, anyway. They escaped from the incident without a scratch when one of them managed to bring the van to a halt a little further down the road. But Marco hit his head on the pavement and was killed.

Sticking her neck out

Isadora Duncan (1877–1927) was an extraordinary dancer, who used an expressive style based on that of the ancient Greeks. Many proponents of the modern dance techniques owe their art to Duncan's tutelage, through the schools she set up near Berlin in 1904, in Paris in 1914 and in Moscow in 1921.

It was while travelling in a car that the life of California-born Dora Angela Duncan (Isadora's real name) was cut short in dramatic fashion. She had been wearing a scarf of Doctor Who proportions, which had become entangled in the spokes of the back wheel of the car. She was strangled and her neck was broken.

Losing their heads

On a warm and sunny day in August 1997 a group of Dutch employees were enjoying a day tour provided by their company. While travelling on the bus some of them decided to stick their heads out of the skylight in the roof and . . . Well, you can guess the rest.

So bracing was the rush of the wind and the sound in their ears, that they ignored several warnings from the bus driver to stop. Two men were singing with their heads stuck out of this skylight when *wham*! The bus passed under a viaduct, and the sickly sounds of breaking bone could be heard throughout the vehicle.

The driver is reported to have told the authorities, 'I always lock the damn thing [skylight] when kids are in the bus, because kids just don't listen. But, for God's sake, these were adults!'

Oh treacherous servant

In Boise, Idaho, a woman in her nineties died after her own car ran over her.

Ethel Smith had apparently forgotten to put the 1973 Dodge Dart into 'park' mode when she pulled up next to a dumpster truck hear her home. She got out of the car – and it promptly ran over her . . . twice.

Paramedics who attended the incident noticed that the wheels were turned, and they believed that the car went in a circle, running over the hapless old woman a second time before bystanders were able to stop it.

Shear stupidity

They're handy things, pruning shears, but like most things, they can be put to inappropriate use.

In Hillsboro, Oregon, in May 2001, a twenty-five-year-old truck driver called Ismael was driving along in his Toyota when he had a collision with a postbox, which caused him to hit an electricity pole. The two crashes sent the truck on to its side and left a power cable draped over the vehicle.

Ismael clambered out of the overturned truck holding a pair of pruning shears in his hands. Police say he very likely used the shears to clip the power cable that was lying across the Toyota.

When the shears touched the 7,500-volt cable, the current, said police, travelled across his heart and out through his left leg, and he was found lying face down on the power line with the shears still in his hands. A lucky passenger survived.

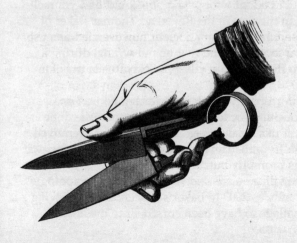

Death in Religious Circumstances

Though practitioners of religion say they love life, it's amazing how many deaths can occur in religious circumstances – and that's not counting the Inquisition

Missionary imposition

You have to be so careful when visiting foreign lands. Put a foot wrong, and you could find yourself dead. In the case of the Reverend Thomas Baker of the London Missionary Society, however, it wasn't so much a foot as a hand that he put wrong, during a visit to the mountain village of Navatusila in Fiji in 1867.

Unfortunately for the missionary, he was unaware that touching the head of a chief was not the done thing in this Fijian village and, so when he removed a comb from the chief's hair, purely out of curiosity, he was promptly butchered to death.

The villagers are said to have offered an apology as recently as 2003 to Baker's descendants, believing their village to have been cursed since the holy man's death.

By name and by nature

He was a Christian and was
even called Christian. In his
devoutness, however, Dennis
Christian of London had
convinced himself that God
would save him if he stepped
off the balcony of his
thirteenth-floor flat. This didn't
happen, of course, and he fell
to his death.

The coroner's inquest was
told that his faith had not –
certainly in this world –
proved triumphant.

Potion lotion notion

If you want to be bulletproof – literally – just cover
yourself in some gloop. That's what tribesmen in
northern Ghana in 2001 evidently thought when one of
them, twenty-three-year-old Aleobiga, and fifteen of
his pals bought a 'magical' potion that was supposedly
capable of withstanding bullets.

They smeared the stuff over their bodies for a
fortnight, after which time Aleobiga volunteered to be
the guinea pig for the Big Test. Instead of asking his
friends to test it on a part of his body that wasn't
essential for living, he stood in a clearing and told
them to shoot him.

They did.

He died.

The man who sold the dodgy nostrum was beaten
for his error of judgement.

Window on the (next) world

Preaching and singing from a high window can upset the neighbours. The American soul singer and songwriter Donnie Hathaway (1946–79) had been in the habit of leaning out of the window of his seventeenth-storey apartment in Chicago, preaching his hot gospel and singing to people below. However, he discovered how unpopular this could be when he was evicted from several hotels for providing this impromptu 'entertainment'.

It didn't deter him, though, for one day he was leaning out of the window on the fifteenth floor of the Essex Hotel in New York, singing and preaching, when he fell to his death.

The incident was ruled as suicide, but when Jesse Jackson gave a eulogy at Hathaway's funeral he pointed out that the singer had been dressed in a coat and scarf at the time, and reasoned that people do not get dressed up 'just to jump out a window'.

Fatal faith

In October 2000, a female member of a Jehovah's Witnesses' splinter group decided to spread the word among motorists, but she chose to do it by standing among the traffic and trying to convert the occupants of the passing vehicles.

Situated in the middle of Interstate 55 in Illinois, she was, of course, hit by a vehicle and killed. Apparently, it was not her first attempt at spreading the word in the middle of the road, but it was definitely her last.

Curse of the Screen

We were surprised by how many of the deaths we had researched were influenced by television and film – enough, anyway, to provide a section of their own. Some people were watching TV, some influenced by something they saw on the large screen, and some were just fixing a TV mains cable.

I'm dying to tell ya

The only compensation for bragging that you're going to live to be a hundred years old, and then being spectacularly proved wrong, is that you're not there to endure the embarrassment. Jerome Irving Rodale did just that.

The seventy-two-year-old creator of a US magazine called *Organic Farming and Gardening* and founder of a major publication corporation, Rodale Press, he was recording a TV interview for *The Dick Cavett Show* in January 1971, discussing the benefits of organic foods, when he declared, 'I'm going to live to be a hundred unless I'm run down by a sugar-crazed taxi driver.'

Unfortunately, the interview had barely reached the halfway stage when Rodale dropped dead in his chair, having suffered a fatal heart attack.

Hot-wired

The *Glasgow Herald* of 28 March 2003 tells the intriguing story of a sixty-four-year-old electrician in Malaga, Spain, who devised his own 'orgasmatron', named after a sex machine in the 1973 Woody Allen film *Sleeper*. Skipping over the finer details, suffice it to say that it had a vibrating mat, massage pads and electrodes to attach to various dangly bits.

A police spokesperson told the media, 'Unfortunately, there seems to have been a power surge while he was watching a film called *Hot Vixen Nuns*. And the flat was damp.'

Given the nature of the film he was watching, which way went the power surge: from the mains to him or from him to the mains? Whichever way it was, the poor man was electrocuted – but it should be safe to assume that he died with a smile on his face.

Political suicide

In the mid-1980s, R. Bud Dwyer was a Pennsylvania state treasurer, but he'd been caught up in some sleaze. He'd been convicted of receiving kickbacks and could have gone to jail for a maximum of fifty-five years, as well as having to pay a huge fine, and on top of that he'd have to resign.

To avoid all that unpleasantness, however, Dwyer decided on a spectacular way of avoiding his troubles for ever. On 22 January 1987 he called a press conference at his office in Harrisburg, which was attended by TV crews and about thirty members of the press. They assumed they were there to witness the announcement of Dwyer's resignation, but they were in for a surprise.

During this live broadcast, Dwyer read from a prepared statement, and grew increasingly nervous and sweaty as his speech went on. After a while, some camera crews began to pack up, but Dwyer warned them that they ought to stay in case they missed something that they'd kick themselves for not having recorded.

He was dead right – in fact he was right dead, too, because after handing out sealed envelopes to his staff, he produced a .357 Magnum and, despite desperate pleas from reporters, he cocked the weapon, stuck the barrel in his mouth and pulled the trigger.

Not a pretty sight . . .

Out of the frying pan . . .

You don't have to be watching or appearing on TV to qualify for this section: you can also be repairing one.

Michael Anderson Godwin had escaped the electric chair, but ended up dying by the very means he had evaded. Stupid, really. He'd spent several years on Death Row and would have gone to South Carolina's electric chair, had his sentence not been commuted to life in prison.

But in March 1989, as he sat on a metal toilet in his cell trying to fix his small TV set, he bit into a wire – and was electrocuted.

A similar thing happened in January 1997 to Laurence Baker, also once on Death Row as a convicted murderer, but subsequently serving a life sentence in the state prison in Pittsburgh. He was zapped by homemade earphones as he sat on his metal toilet watching TV.

No Laughing Matter

What a way to go, eh? Tommy Cooper did it, dying (in the literal sense) on stage, and others have died laughing, too, as these rib-tickling accounts testify.

Ee, by eck!

Ask anyone which episode they remember most from *The Goodies* – that wacky TV comedy of the seventies – and they'll probably tell you it's the episode called 'The Lancastrian Martial Art of Ecky Thump'. Ecky thump was the Northern British version of kung fu, of course, and the whole episode was done as a spoof of the *Kung Fu* TV series of the time. Who can forget seeing Bill Oddie in the tin bath, the washerwoman pouring Vim or Ajax on him, and the voiceover talking of how he was being cleansed in 'exotic unguents'?

It was especially funny for fifty-year-old Alex Mitchell, a Kings Lynn brickie, who was sitting watching it with his wife Nessie, when he burst into a fit of uncontrollable laughter. For half an hour Alex shook with hysteria, eventually dying of a heart attack.

Nessie, it is said, later wrote to the programme makers to thank them for making Alex's last half-hour such a happy one.

Keep the rats away

All but the most ascetic of us must have wished at
some time that we could, literally, die laughing. Not
right now, of course, but rather when the appointed
hour comes, and the Reaper stands, scythe by his
side, regarding us balefully from the blackness of his
eye sockets, the characteristic rictus grin just visible in
the folds of his terrible hood. Oh, to laugh in his face!
Pietro Aretino (1492–1556) managed to die laughing,
however, although whether he actually saw the grim
figure of the Reaper it's impossible to ascertain.

This Italian poet was known to be one of the
wittiest men of his time, and often caused scandals
with his satirical, bawdy comedies. He was even
banished from his native town of Arezzo for writing
a satirical poem on papal indulgences. He moved to
Rome, but, after publishing some lewd sonnets, he
was kicked out of that city, too.

One day at the age of sixty-four, however, he
became convulsed with laughter at a joke – a dirty
one, of course – and died of an apoplectic fit.

A priest was called and smeared some 'holy' oil
on his forehead, and with his last breath Aretino is
said to have told his gathered friends, 'Keep the rats
away now I'm all greased up' – a funny man until
the very end.

Painted lady

The Greek painter Zeuxis had just completed a portrait of an old woman, but he wasn't happy with it. The brushwork was all wrong. However, instead of cursing he began to chuckle. And he chuckled some more. And some more.

Before long, Zeuxis – who flourished in Athens during the fifth century BCE – was laughing uncontrollably, so much so, so one story has it, that it led to his death.

Good golly, Miss Polly!

Mirth and woe are the strangest of bedfellows, but they come together more often than we might think, as shown by this tale of how laughter led to demise.

This was the turn of one Mrs Fitzherbert from Northamptonshire, who, on a Wednesday evening in April 1782, went to see *The Beggar's Opera* at the Drury Lane Theatre. What tickled this merry widow, it seems, were the antics of the actor Mr Bannister, who was dressed as Polly Peachum. So amusing was Mr Bannister's performance that the whole audience were doubled over in laughter.

But it got to Mrs Fitzherbert more than the rest. She was so consumed by the humour of the spectacle that she had to leave the theatre, and couldn't get it off her mind. Every time she brought the image to her mind, she would collapse in a fit of laughter.

An issue of *Gentlemen's Magazine* – published a week later – completes the story: 'Not being able to banish the figure from her memory, she was thrown into hysterics, which continued without intermission until she expired Friday morning.'

Donkey ho ho ho tee hee hee

Chrysippus (279–207 BCE) was one of the Stoics of Greek philosophy. But he had a weakness, it seems: he couldn't stop laughing.

All kinds of things made him laugh, so much so that he needed all the stoicism he could muster to keep himself from laughing himself to death, and he didn't manage that for long, it would seem.

The cause of his final bout of mirth was the sight of his donkey eating figs. It was just too much for the hapless Greek.

Ice and easy does it

Just when you thought there couldn't possibly be yet another story about someone who's laughed himself to death, we present the story of the driver of an ice-cream truck in Thailand who, in 2003, died while laughing – in his sleep.

Fifty-two-year-old Damnoen Saen-um, from Phrae province, 300 miles (483 km) north of Bangkok, laughed for about two minutes and then stopped breathing, according to *The Nation*, which quoted officials. His wife tried to wake him, but he just kept laughing. A post-mortem suggested he may have had a heart attack.

Dr Somchai Chakrabhand, deputy director-general of the Mental Health Department, is quoted in *The Nation* as saying, 'I have never seen a case like this. But it is possible that a person could have heart seizure while laughing or crying too hard in their sleep.'

All Michael O'Mara titles are available by post from:
Bookpost, PO Box 29, Douglas, Isle of Man, IM99 1BQ

Credit cards accepted. Telephone: 01624 677237   Fax: 01624 670923
Email: bookshop@enterprise.net Internet: www.bookpost.co.uk

Free postage and packing in the UK.

Other Michael O'Mara Humour titles:

The Book of Urban Legends – ISBN 1-85479-932-0 pb £3.99
Born for the Job – ISBN 1-84317-099-X pb £5.99
The Complete Book of Farting – ISBN 1-85479-440-X pb £4.99
The Ultimate Insult – ISBN 1-85479-288-1 pb £5.99
Wicked Cockney Rhyming Clang ICDN 1-05479-00C-1 pb £3.99
The Wicked Wit of Jane Austen – ISBN 1-85479-652-6 hb £9.99
The Wicked Wit of Winston Churchill – ISBN 1-85479-529-5 hb £9.99
The Wicked Wit of Oscar Wilde – ISBN 1-85479-542-2 hb £9.99
The World's Stupidest Laws – ISBN 1-84317-172-4 pb £4.99
The World's Stupidest Signs – ISBN 1-84317-170-8 pb £4.99
More of the World's Stupidest Signs – ISBN 1-84317-032-9 pb £4.99
The World's Stupidest Last Words – ISBN 1-84317-021-3 pb £4.99
The World's Stupidest Inventions – ISBN 1-84317-036-1 pb £5.99
The World's Stupidest Instructions – ISBN 1-84317-078-7 pb £4.99
The World's Stupidest Sporting Screw-Ups – ISBN 1-84317-039-6 pb £4.99
The World's Stupidest Chat-Up Lines – ISBN 1-84317-019-1 pb £4.99
The World's Stupidest Headlines – ISBN 1-84317-105-8 pb £4.99
The World's Stupidest Criminals – ISBN 1-84317-171-6 pb £4.99
The World's Stupidest Husbands – ISBN 1-84317-168-6 pb £4.99
Cricket: It's A Funny Old Game – ISBN 1-84317-090-6 pb £4.99
Football: It's A Funny Old Game – ISBN 1-84317-091-4 pb £4.99
Laughable Latin – ISBN 1-84317-097-3 pb £4.99
School Rules – ISBN 1-84317-100-7 pb £4.99
Sex Cheques (new edition) – ISBN 1-84317-121-X pb £3.50
The Timewaster Letters – ISBN 1-84317-108-2 pb £9.99
The Jordan Joke Book – ISBN 1-84317-120-1 pb £4.99
Speak Well English – ISBN 1-84317-088-4 pb £5.99
Shite's Unoriginal Miscellany – ISBN 1-84317-064-7 hb £9.99
Eats, Shites & Leaves – ISBN 1-84317-098-1 hb £9.99
A Shite History of Nearly Everything – ISBN 1-84317-138-4 hb £9.99